CW01663199

PRAISE FOR
THE HOPE OF A THOUSAND HILLS

"This book is an eloquent and moving testimony to God's miraculous work of reconciliation, taking place amidst the deepest fracture and desolation. It is the story of individuals and communities who are at once ordinary and extraordinary: human beings for whom deep suffering makes reconciliation intensely painful, but who have somehow summoned the courage to allow God to transform their wounds and their lives. It is also the story of women and men who have followed God's lead, allowing reconciliation to overflow from person to person and nation to nation. The Women on the Frontline reconciliation programme in the Anglican Communion had the privilege of partnering with Joseph Nyamutera in South Sudan. It was inspiring to see the power of 'Healing the Wounds of Ethnic Conflict' to begin a new journey of reconciliation, unleashing unexpected, vibrant hope. I pray that this book will kindle in each of us not only admiration but the deep calling to live the gospel of reconciliation ourselves."

Justin Welby, Archbishop of Canterbury

"Emily Bankhead's recounting of this beautiful work of reconciliation warms the soul. These stories need to be told, as they enlarge our view of God's healing power and grace, and indirectly challenge us in how we deal with our own hurts and issues. Out of the depths of Rwanda's darkness, Jesus' light has brought hope and new life that sometimes defies belief."

Simon Guillebaud, Great Lakes Outreach, Burundi

"I am so pleased this book has been written at this time. We need to do all we can to support the growth of knowledge and understanding of the issues related to the 1994 genocide, and to encourage other peoples and nations to work towards reconciliation. My work with The Rwandan Sisterhood has opened my eyes to the powerful progress this beautiful country continues to make."

Dame Helen Hyde DBE

THE HOPE OF A THOUSAND HILLS

THE HOPE OF A THOUSAND HILLS

A Story of Healing and Reconciliation in Rwanda, and Beyond

Emily Bankhead

First published in Great Britain in 2018 by Selwyn Shore

Copyright © 2018 Emily Bankhead

All rights reserved. Except for brief excerpts for review purposes, no part of this book may be reproduced or used in any form without written permission from the publisher.

Scripture taken from the Holy Bible, NEW INTERNATIONAL VERSION®, NIV® Copyright © 1973, 1978, 1984, 2011 by Biblica, Inc.® Used by permission. All rights reserved worldwide. NEW INTERNATIONAL VERSION® and NIV® are registered trademarks of Biblica, Inc. Use of either trademark for the offering of goods or services requires the prior written consent of Biblica US, Inc.

ISBN: 978-1-9993301-0-1
eISBN: 978-1-9993301-1-8

Cover design by Matt Withers
Typeset by Thirteen Creative

"Now to him who is able to do immeasurably more than all we ask or imagine, according to his power that is at work within us, to him be glory in the church and in Christ Jesus throughout all generations, for ever and ever."

Ephesians 3:20-21

Contents

Preface

It was in Rubavu, a north-western district of Rwanda, that I experienced a rainstorm like no other. We had to shout to make ourselves heard. It was powerful, thunderous and fierce. It drowned everything else out and stopped us in our tracks. It was unrelenting and awesome.

My husband and I were meeting with some friends from Rabagirana Ministries (formerly Mercy Ministries International Great Lakes) to learn about their outreach work in rebuilding the communities of Rubavu amidst the ongoing reverberations of the appalling genocide of 1994. We had been connected with Joseph Nyamutera of Rabagirana through his long-standing friendship with my father-in-law and had had a tantalising glimpse, over the years, into some of the incredible restoration that has been experienced since those one hundred horrifying days.

Right from the start, we were captivated by the glory of God overflowing from this small, fertile land that sits squeezed between DRC, Uganda, Tanzania and Burundi in the heart of the African continent. It was clear that these testimonies, the revolutionary ministry of Dr. Rhiannon Lloyd and African Evangelistic Enterprise (AEE), the unceasing efforts of Joseph and the Rabagirana team, and the impact of the wider Healing the Wounds of Ethnic Conflict (HWEC) movement, must be told and must be heard.

And as I worked through this project and re-lived the testimonies, and especially as I listened back to my recording of that conversation in Rubavu and tried to make sense of the words above the cacophony of the thundering rain, this is something that kept coming back to me: however loudly the pain roars, God's love is louder, more fierce, more powerful. There is nothing – not the deepest loss nor the most resounding pain – that can ever drown it out.

One thing that is clear from every heart-wrenching testimony is that healing and reconciliation is not an easy process, and it doesn't come cheap. It is painful to the core, gruelling, messy and draining. But through it and over and above it all, like the rain, the love of God thunders.

Much has been said and written about the unimaginable depravity, pain and destruction of the Rwandan genocide, but you only have to encounter a handful of courageous Rwandans who are willing to share their experiences of healing and restoration to find that these stories shout louder. The glorious truth that overflows from the borders of Rwanda today is that for every horror that is inflicted and every injustice that is suffered, there is a greater, more powerful story waiting in the wings. There is a voice that cries out in the wilderness. There is a light that extinguishes the dark.

This book is not intended to be a historical account of the genocide, nor an analysis of the factors that brought it about – for this, I would recommend Gerard Prunier's The Rwanda Crisis, 1959-1994: History of a Genocide (Fountain Publishers, Kampala; 1995). Rather, the aim is to shout from the top of Rwanda's "thousand hills" that no situation is too hopeless to be redeemed, and no heart is too broken to be restored. My hope is that you will be inspired by the resilience of the Rwandan people, and the extraordinary and extravagant healing power of God, that you will be encouraged by the reality that God is able to make new the most broken hearts and lives, and that you will feel empowered and equipped to be instruments of this same healing and reconciliation potential in whatever context you find yourself. Above all, this is a testimony to the capacity of God to do more than we dare to imagine: to bring hope out of despair, love out of hate, and peace out of conflict. To multiply our meagre offerings and use them to change the world.

Twenty years ago, Rwanda bore witness to some of the worst that humanity is capable of, and the world turned its face away. Today, by the grace of God, and the strength and faith of the Rwandan people, she is becoming a beacon of hope, a light for the nations, reflecting the very glory of God. We cannot afford to look away this time.

Emily Bankhead
Manchester, 2018

Introduction

Diversity is a part of Rwanda's rich heritage – it is in the soil, the roots, and the air – but in the wrong hands, almost anything can be turned into a deadly weapon. Long before a mzungu ("white man") set foot on Rwandan soil, these lush green hills were home to the Hutu, the Tutsi and the Twa. To call these "ethnic groups", though, is something of an over-simplification, an attempt to force them into a structure that the western world can understand. This was the fatal mistake made by the first white colonisers. In fact, the people of Rwanda all speak the same language and share the same culture, and before the Europeans arrived there was no strict distinction between them.

The colonial rulers drew divisions along mostly superficial lines and exploited these differences in order to maintain power and control over the population. Based, for the most part, on appearance and apparent wealth (number of livestock), the Tutsis were favoured and elevated into the more powerful positions, while the majority Hutu population was oppressed. In 1933, identity cards were introduced, making these ethnic "labels" official.

In 1959, independence came to Rwanda in the form of a violent and bloody Hutu revolution, in the name of majority rule, which was legitimised with elections in 1963. Outbreaks of violence and retaliation continued, and thousands of Tutsis were already fleeing the country. Between 1990 and 1993, civil war raged between the Rwandan Patriotic Front (RPF) and the Hutu government.

By early 1994, there was widespread propaganda against the Tutsis on radio and TV channels, playing on an underlying resentment over years of Tutsi privilege, and the fear of what might happen if Hutus didn't fight back. On 6 April, a plane carrying both the Rwandan and Burundi presidents was shot down, and this acted as a trigger for full scale genocide against the Tutsis – militia, politicians and civilians alike. Initially orchestrated by government officials and Hutu militia (Interahamwe); the thirst for genocide spread to the grassroots level at a horrifying pace. Hundreds of Tutsis were killed in just the first two days, and within a week over ten thousand had been massacred in Kigali alone.

The Rwandan Armed Forces (FAR) and Interahamwe systematically moved from house to house to kill every Tutsi, and set up roadblocks to catch any of those who were attempting to flee. Young Hutu men formed groups and hunted down their Tutsi neighbours and friends – men, women and children – with machetes, iron bars, or whatever they could find. Many moderate Hutus were also killed as they were considered too sympathetic to the Tutsis, and Twa were often seen as collaborators. The frantic and chaotic nature of the genocide makes it difficult to be sure of a death toll, but estimates suggest that between 800,000 and a million Rwandans were killed between April and July.

Two years after the genocide, refugees (predominantly Hutus) started to return from neighbouring countries, and between 2005 and 2007 more than 60,000 prisoners – perpetrators of the genocide – were released. These people returned to their communities to live alongside their Tutsi neighbours, alongside the families and friends of their victims. The commandment to "Love your neighbour" has rarely been so bluntly and brutally tested, and yet little was done to re-integrate these people back into the community and to acknowledge the tensions this stirred up. The nation has been rebuilt on the premise of a unified identity – "You are no longer Tutsi, Hutu or Twa. We are all Rwandans!" – but pain, guilt, shame and fear don't just dissolve with time.

If Rwandans are to proclaim "never again" with any real confidence and assurance, superficial peace is not enough. Healing Rwanda's wounds of ethnic conflict must surely start with healing the wounds of individual Rwandans. Only then can communities, churches and the government work together, hand in hand, to confront the roots of conflict, reinforce communities for future generations, and build peace into the very fabric of society.

This is the basis on which the HWEC movement was initiated by Rhiannon Lloyd and African Evangelistic Enterprise, soon joined by Joseph and MMI. Now Rabagirana Ministries, the vision of MMI remains the same: that Rwanda would become a source of lasting peace, unity and light for the nations, to the glory of God (Isaiah 60:1-3). This is not just a hope or a dream, but a mission that is being practically worked out and sought after in communities across the nation. Neighbours who once turned against each other with homemade nail-studded clubs are now standing side by side, rebuilding their homes, families and communities with bare hands and healed hearts.

This is a story of God's healing and reconciliation of the Rwandan people, which began just months after the killing ended. It has since grown into a far-reaching movement, bringing together churches, government leaders, international organisations and individuals from all over the world under the banner of Healing the Wounds of Ethnic Conflict. This is also a story of the possibility and the power of forgiveness. It is a story of God's capacity to heal, reconcile and restore. It is a story for all of us, and this is just the beginning.

CHAPTER ONE

He Multiplies Small Offerings

Between April and June 1994, more than 10% of Rwanda's population had been killed, and a further 30% had retreated into exile. The genocide left in its wake a nation in complete shock and disarray, and deeply traumatised. Homes, schools, churches and public buildings had been looted, burned or demolished, and much of the country's infrastructure was destroyed. There was a lack of running water and electricity, few functional vehicles, and a severe labour shortage. Corpses were stacked in the streets, many survivors were gravely injured, and some were still hiding in the hills. Close to 114,000 children had been orphaned. More than ever, the people of Rwanda needed to come together to rebuild their beautiful country with their hands, from the ground up. But how could they stand alongside their neighbours? How could they look them in the eye? Who could they trust? Shock, trauma, guilt, denial and fear reigned over the "land of a thousand hills", and it seemed that the darkness had won.

THE CALL

It was into this darkness that God called an unlikely servant. Dr. Rhiannon Lloyd, a medical doctor and psychiatrist, had worked with Medair (a Christian NGO) in Liberia in 1992, offering trauma counselling and training for orphanage staff. She received a phone call from Medair in September 1994, inviting her to join them in Rwanda to work with the pastors and churches. With only two weeks available in her schedule, Rhiannon eventually agreed on a short visit, but as she read and learned more about the genocide, in preparation for her trip, she began to regret her decision. She was horrified by what she discovered, and felt utterly out of her depth: "What could anyone do in a country where everyone was severely traumatised, let alone one little Welsh woman?!"

The night before she was due to leave, Rhiannon was in such a panic that she couldn't even bring herself to pack her bag, but God was determined to get her on the plane. A friend came to her door and told her that the Holy Spirit had prompted her to come and pray with Rhiannon, and to remind her of the story of the feeding of the five thousand (Matthew 14:31-21). Through the gentle encouragement of a friend, and the powerful testimony of scripture, God spoke straight to Rhiannon's heart: "Rhiannon, I am still God, and I still know how to multiply insignificant offerings." Weeping, she knew that she must go, with whatever little she had to offer.

INTO THE SHADOW OF GENOCIDE

During her initial two-week visit to devastated Rwanda, God called His willing servant to the town of Nyamata, in the region of Bugesera, in the south of the country. The name of the area means "curse" or "calamity" and it is renowned for its droughts. It had also been the scene of many bloody wars between Rwanda and Burundi. The region used to be a semi-arid savannah where pregnant girls and bandits were exiled to die. In the violence of 1959, those Tutsis who were not killed were driven into a part of Bugesera where the tsetse fly swarmed, so that many died of disease. Moreover, every time Tutsi exiles tried to fight their way back into Rwanda, the Tutsis in Bugesera paid a heavy price. This was the worst affected area during the genocide of 1994, with almost 80% of the population being killed.

Rhiannon remembers her first impressions of Nyamata when she arrived in September 1994, just weeks after the genocide had been brought to an end:

> The smell of death was everywhere. Churches were bloodstained, some still containing the unburied bodies of the victims. I looked into the empty eyes of a greatly diminished population that had lost hope. We drove through empty villages, whose inhabitants were either dead or had fled. Orphans pined for lost parents; parents pined for lost children. But mostly it seemed people were numb – in a state of shock: "How could this have happened? How could he/she have done this? And he was an elder in the church...!" I encountered fear, pain, anger, disbelief, but most of all, hopelessness. I cried out to God: "Do You have hope for this situation? If not, I may as well go home. I have to know what You feel!"

She met with various church groups and listened to the seemingly endless and indescribably desolating stories. She found that many pastors were questioning whether forgiveness and reconciliation would ever be possible. At this point, such healing just seemed so out of reach. The people Rhiannon met were utterly traumatised, and even talking about forgiveness seemed hugely disrespectful. There were already many secular and Christian groups offering trauma counselling by this time, but many people were unresponsive and unwilling to share their pain, as this was counter-cultural to them. When someone preached about forgiveness, people tended to get angry, and understandably so: "Don't you realise how much I've suffered? I've lost my whole family, and you're saying I should forgive?"

AT THE FOOT OF THE CROSS

Completely overwhelmed, and wondering what she could possibly tell these people to begin to heal their hearts, Rhiannon was reminded of what God had done to heal her own life's hurts, and felt convicted that His nature is the same in every circumstance, for all time. Hesitantly and warily, she started to share some key principles that had helped her, and the people who heard her speak were blessed. Incredibly, they started to believe that God's healing might just be possible for their nation, too. Rhiannon shared her belief that the only way forward was to come together, at the foot of the cross; that this was the only thing powerful enough, and good enough, to overcome such evil.

After her brief but transformative visit in September, Rhiannon returned to Rwanda in June 1995 to partner with African Evangelistic Enterprise. The initial plan was for her to train orphanage staff and counsellors, because of her experience in Liberia, but it quickly became clear that traditional counselling was not the way forward. It was neither culturally accepted as a practice, nor relevant and helpful in speaking to the depths of the reality of the Rwandan people's trauma. Rhiannon realised that it was not possible to teach on forgiveness, or even to talk about forgiveness, until people had first been to the cross and released their hearts from all the pain they were carrying around. Healing and forgiveness can only start from a revelation of who God is: despite what we see around us, and however dark, depraved and broken the world may become, God's heart and character never change. As she sought God's guidance, Rhiannon was reminded of Romans 15:13: "May the God of hope fill you with all joy and peace as you trust in him, so that you may overflow with hope by the power of the Holy Spirit." He is the God of hope and He cannot be otherwise. Wherever He is, there is hope; even in a country reeling from genocide.

THE CHURCH AS AN AGENT OF HEALING

Very early on, Rhiannon became convinced that the Church was the agent that God would use to bring healing in Rwanda: "1 John 3:8 tells us that 'the reason the Son of God appeared was to destroy the devil's work.' As we are His body on earth now, that is our work too." She began to meet with groups of Christians with this message that they must now take on the mantle of being the light of the world. But the Church in Rwanda had suffered a crisis during the genocide, and it quickly became clear that the pastors felt they were in no position to lead the people on a journey of healing and forgiveness.

It is natural to look to the Church for hope in the midst of grief and healing in the wake of trauma, but what if she is silent – or worse? This is the question that has weighed on pastors, Christians and non-Christians alike since the events of 1994: where was the Church during the genocide? The Church was not immune to the "ethnic issue"; even if some priests and pastors held back from actively taking part in the killings, there was prejudice and division before the genocide, and hatred and suspicion afterwards. The church buildings themselves had not been safe places of refuge during the killings – far from it. In the Sainte-Famille Church in downtown Kigali, thousands took refuge, only to be picked off by the militia, with the help of members of the clergy. Tragically, this was not an isolated case. Gérard Prunier writes, in The Rwanda Crisis, 1959-1994: History of a Genocide (Fountain Publishers, Kampala; 1995): "Although…there were admirable acts of courage among ordinary Christians, the church hierarchies were at best useless and at worst accomplices in the genocide." The sad truth is that the Church in Rwanda wasn't just a powerless bystander but a contributing factor to the horrors that unfolded and, in some cases, an active participant.

Painfully aware of the Church's failures, weaknesses and woundedness, the pastors and leaders that Rhiannon met with would often become crestfallen and despondent, saying: "No, we have lost our credibility. Some parts of the Church participated in the genocide. There is nothing we can say now." Seeing how hopeless and defeated they were, Rhiannon felt anger stir in her spirit. She realised that, if it was God's strategy to use His Church to be a light to the country, it was the devil's strategy to use the failure of some to discredit the whole. This only made her more convinced, and more determined, that the way forward was to target the pastors.

THE WORKSHOPS

AEE became the initial umbrella for this ministry, since the organization was already known for its burden for reconciliation. The head of AEE Rwanda, Israel Havugimana, had been martyred during the genocide for speaking out against the killings, and three of the seven staff members were also murdered. Havugimana's successor was Antoine Rutayisire, an Anglican pastor who later also became chairman of the National Unity and Reconciliation Commission. AEE had the reputation, and Antoine already had the heart, but Rhiannon brought a systematic teaching series that would provide the form and structure of the reconciliation work.

The workshops were called "Healing the Wounds of Ethnic Conflict (HWEC)" and invited the Holy Spirit to lead participants through a series of principles, with each session building on the ones before. It was clear that a strong and solid groundwork must be laid before people could risk opening up their heart wounds, so the workshops started with the only sure foundation: the love of God. Understanding God's heart, His feelings, attitudes and unchanging character, and how He felt about the genocide, became the basis of the HWEC workshops. From there, participants were led to the cross: the place of personal healing, as well as forgiveness.

Facilitating workshops, Rhiannon was joined by Anastase Sabamungu, a Tutsi pastor who had been brought up in exile in Uganda, and many of whose family members had been brutally killed in the genocide. Later, they were also joined by Joseph Nyamutera, a Hutu former school teacher who, fearing indiscriminate mass reprisals after the genocide, had fled the country with his family and had suffered greatly in a refugee camp in Zaire (now, The Democratic Republic of Congo). Anastase and Joseph were from backgrounds that were as divided and antagonistic as could be, but they believed that coming together in this ministry was part of God's strategy. Many of those who attended the workshops have said that they began to find healing even before Anastase and Joseph opened their mouths: just seeing the two of them standing there together, clearly in good relationship, leading a workshop on reconciliation, was powerful and transformative enough. They both brought their own invaluable insights and contributed greatly to the workshop, as well as being living examples of healing and reconciliation.

Under AEE, the team began travelling around the country and conducting the workshops in every major town. In the beginning, the message of healing and reconciliation was taken to as many churches as possible, but as time went on they were invited to hold HWEC workshops for other organisations, and to expand their reach. As the ministry grew, more and more opportunities opened up for the teaching to be heard; including speeches on the radio, workshops in schools and universities, and even gatherings in football stadiums. Church and community leaders were trained as facilitators so that they could form regional teams and run their own healing workshops. The seed that God had planted in the inglorious town of Nyamata soon grew, bloomed and spread across the country, with teams in Butare, Byumba, Cyangugu, Gikongoro, Gisenyi, Gitarama, Kibungo, Kibuye, Ruhengeri and Mutara. As Antoine stressed, there was not a person in Rwanda who did not need this workshop: "There is no Rwandan who has not been affected by the genocide; if not directly, then by its consequences."

A NEW PHASE

Two years after the HWEC workshops started, they came up against new challenges and dimensions. In 1996, many refugees began to return to Rwanda from DRC and Tanzania so that genocide survivors and perpetrators, and their families and neighbours, were once again brought face to face. The HWEC team prayed for the peaceful return of these refugees, and miraculously there was very little open violence, but it was unavoidable that this new context posed a further challenge for the work of healing and reconciliation.

As refugees started to pour back into the country, so too did much of the underlying tension and fear that had been kept at bay, waiting in the wings. All of a sudden, healing and forgiveness was being put to the ultimate test. As one survivor pointedly admits: "It is one thing to say you forgive your neighbour when he is dying of cholera in another country; it is another thing altogether when he comes back to live next door." The HWEC team prayed that, in each town, those who had responded well during the workshops would take the lead in receiving back the refugees. By God's inconceivable power and grace, in the next follow-up workshops they heard some wonderful stories of mercy and forgiveness towards the refugees.

A new phase of the ministry was launched, in which genocide survivors and returnees from the camps were now to be brought together in workshops. Again, the team began to travel around the country but, inevitably, the work had become much harder, cloaked in tension and suspicion. It was only the level ground at the foot of the cross that was powerful enough to make the difference. In fact, the healing that people found at the cross seemed even deeper than before, and the subsequent worship would often continue into the early hours of the morning.

There was still a mountain to climb, but the very first steps towards real healing and reconciliation could be seen and felt. In 1996, after the peaceful return of the refugees, a rally was held in the national football stadium, attended by both government and church leaders, to give thanks to God. Antoine declared that the peaceful return of the refugees had been a miracle, a work of God in answer to prayer. One official mockingly said, "If it is God, ask Him to do something about the prisons. They are full of guilty people who are denying their involvement in the genocide!" Seeing this as an opportunity and an invitation, Antoine lost no time in setting up a prayer network to intercede for the prisons, asking the Holy Spirit to come and convict people of sin, and to turn many hearts to the Lord.

For some time, there seemed to be only a limited answer to this prayer. After Bishop Desmond Tutu had come to Rwanda from South Africa in 1995, and sent someone to preach in the prisons, the government saw some real change through repentance, and were moved to open the prison gates for more Christian leaders to preach about repentance and forgiveness. AEE, and other evangelists and pastors, went on slowly and faithfully bringing the gospel to those in the prisons. On one occasion, after Antoine had preached, an inmate spontaneously burst out in confession. Other prisoners followed his lead, and they finally had to end the session after four hours. When they went back to the prison the following week, 800 prisoners confessed their atrocities. In 1998, Antoine went to Kibungo prison, where two thousand people confessed and most gave their lives to Christ.

In 2003, a law was put in place granting partial amnesty to those who confessed their involvement in the genocide. All of a sudden, large-scale repentance began to sweep the country. News flooded in of thousands who had repented and confessed their crimes. Of course, not everyone who confessed had truly come under the conviction of the Holy Spirit; some merely wanted lighter sentences and, once they were released from prison, denied their confession. However, a significant number of those who confessed appear to have done so through finding salvation, or returning to faith.

A DROP IN THE OCEAN

The message of healing and reconciliation has sometimes taken different formats, and the three-day workshop is not feasible in every context, but what has always been clear is that any genuine healing and repentance must start at the foot of the cross, and is only possible through the power of the cross.

When Rhiannon was first called to Rwanda, she felt she had nothing significant to offer, and that anything she contributed would be a tiny drop in a vast and tumultuous ocean. But God brought together her strategic teaching and Antoine's heart for reconciliation, within the structure and influence of AEE, and magnified this into an unyielding wave, an inexorable current of healing and reconciliation, through the power of the Holy Spirit. Hundreds of thousands of people have now passed through the workshops, or have heard the teachings in rallies or on the radio, and many thousands have received healing, which has enabled them to forgive, be forgiven and be reconciled. Truly, God always knows how to magnify our smallest offerings, and to make them count.

CHAPTER TWO

At the Foot of the Cross

There is no doubt that the powerful, even unimaginable impact of the HWEC workshops, compared to trauma counselling or preaching on forgiveness in isolation, ultimately lies in the fact that the material is rooted in an understanding of God's heart. For many people, such extreme and unjust suffering can cause us to blame God, to rage against Him, to accuse Him or to reject Him, and it makes sense that if we feel that God has played some role in our suffering, we will never be able to find healing in Him. It is also vital, as part of a genuine and deep-rooted healing process, to fully acknowledge and give voice to the wounds that have been inflicted on us and to the things that we have lost. Any other route to healing and reconciliation is likely to be superficial or temporary.

Describing the very deliberate structure of the workshop material, Rhiannon uses the imagery of building a house: there's no point trying to put the roof in place before you have laid firm foundations and built sturdy walls. In the same way, it is very difficult to forgive and be reconciled when the heart is still full of pain; this is the wrong order of events. This kind of "forgiveness" involves burying a lot of pain rather than facing it head on, and choosing to live in peace with your neighbours even though your heart is still broken and bitter.

Reconciliation is the crowning glory of the workshops, but it comes as the fruit of healing and repentance. A lot of work has to be done, on a personal and a collective level, before we can even think of reconciliation.

It is not a simple formula, and no two stories are the same. For many of those who have passed through the workshops it has taken years of painful journeying to get to the point where they can open their hearts to the idea of forgiveness and reconciliation. Many more are still on this journey. However, it is the hope of Rhiannon, AEE, MMI (Rabagirana Ministries), and all those who have been involved in the HWEC workshops that this material will continue to be a powerful starting point and transformative guide in the ministry of healing the wounds of ethnic conflict, all over the world.

LAYING THE FOUNDATION

The workshops begin by considering God's original intention for relationships: what does a restored and healed relationship look like? The Trinity is presented as the perfect model of relationship, and the purest example of unity in diversity. There is perfect love, without competition, and every party is equally valued. No-one feels threatened, everyone is safely held by this love, and each complements the other. This, then, is the model for all relationships: when God said, "Let us make mankind in our image," (Genesis 1:26) He was inviting human beings to share this same quality of relationship. So the question is, what went wrong? The workshops consider how humankind has fallen short of God's plan for human relationships so that, instead of celebrating our diversity, we start to feel threatened by one another. Rather than being a source of enrichment and blessing, ethnicity becomes a thorn in our side.

The second session goes on to address the "bitter roots" of prejudice, and helps participants to understand the dangerous power of harbouring prejudice. There is an invitation and an opportunity for them to identify any prejudices they may be carrying around

– whether consciously or subconsciously – and to admit these to themselves. Such opinions and beliefs might seem harmless, but the aim of this session is to expose both the roots of these views and values, and the awful consequences of leaving them unchecked. In this way, many people become fully aware, for the first time, of firmly entrenched prejudices that have been passed down to them from their families, churches and experiences. Gaudence shares how this part of the workshops particularly impacted her:

> When they arrived at the topic of bitter roots, I discovered that even I, myself, had that bitter root, because I hated Tutsis so much. When they reached the topic of forgiveness, I started crying so much because I realised how much I was wounded by the fact that my father was put in prison because of Tutsis, and I found that I had that hatred for the Tutsi… I realised that all Tutsis are not bad, and that on both sides – Tutsi and Hutu – there are good and bad people. Before, I had some prejudice that all Tutsis are bad, but after this workshop, I realised that everyone is good or bad on his own side.

Similarly, Omer talks about how this teaching renewed his thinking, at a deeply transformative level:

> I had a strong prejudice against Tutsis, but the training helped me to celebrate diversity, to accept others, to see and understand that anyone is capable of doing bad things, whether Tutsi or Hutu. But if we come together and accept one another, we cultivate peace: we can live longer, and we can live in peace.

From this point, the teaching moves on to consider how this new perspective on human relationships and diversity can lead to a restored identity as fellow citizens of God's Holy Nation (1 Peter 2:9). This transcends ethnic identity and is an invitation for all to take their place as equal members, with mutual respect and joy in diversity. We are all part of the body of Christ, and there is no higher identity. This redeemed sense of identity and belonging to the Holy Nation has proven truly freeing for many participants in the workshops. Finding release from past bitterness, and embracing their citizenship in the Holy Nation, also empowers people to take their place as instrumental prophetic voices in their country. Through a renewed mind, they are able to embrace and celebrate diversity, and demonstrate a higher way of living: exchanging prejudice, suspicion and hatred for love, grace and fellowship.

This, in turn, prepares the Church to rise up as God's chosen agent of change. This session focuses on God's plan for His Church to reveal to the world His heart for genuine relationship, regardless of gender, ethnic group, or denomination. As church leaders and members are guided through this material, they begin to see how the Church – in Rwanda and beyond – can be released from its shame and guilt, and receive fresh hope and anointing to be the light of the world.

By this point, many participants may be feeling that this picture of God's heart for human relationships, His Holy Nation, and His hope for the Church are all well and good, but actually being able to trust God after such overwhelming suffering, and to know Him as a God of love, feels like a step too far. With wounds that still feel so fresh and raw, the idea of a good and just God feels too far out of reach. It is important, at this stage of the workshops, to acknowledge and sit with the question of how suffering can undermine our ability to trust God. People must be allowed to voice their doubts and the struggles of their hearts to reconcile such depths of suffering with a good, just and loving God, rather than simply burying or masking these uncomfortable tensions.

Indeed, many godly people in the Bible also had their doubts and struggles (see, for example, Psalm 22:1, 74:1; Habakkuk 1:2) and this helps to validate how we might feel, rather than how we think we should be feeling. No-one could blame or judge those who have endured such extreme suffering as genocide for drawing certain conclusions about God: that He favours some groups over others, that He is the author of suffering, that He is powerless to help, or that He is indifferent to our pain. These are all legitimate feelings, and the workshops give space for these to be acknowledged and expressed, without judgment. Such accusations against God come out of deeply wounded hearts, so theological arguments are not going to be enough to "convince" us, intellectually, that they are false. Instead, we need a revelation from the Holy Spirit about God's true character.

The workshops therefore explore various unchanging truths about God's character, and the ways in which He has revealed Himself to His people over centuries. This is the starting point, through which all of our pain and anger should be filtered and interpreted. When we look at scripture, we cannot deny that God is just and loves justice. He is described as "a faithful God who does no wrong, upright and just is he…" (Deuteronomy 32:4) and His relationship to His people throughout the Old and New Testaments bears this out in action. Based on God's revelation of Himself through His Word and throughout history, we cannot realistically believe that He is the author of injustice. How, then, can we make sense of injustice in the world around us? Again, using scripture as the starting point, the workshops highlight certain truths that help to fully acknowledge the very real existence of evil, injustice and suffering in our world, while reassuring us that this is not the will of God: we all have the freedom to make life choices, whether for good or evil, and sin is not God's will. In fact, Proverbs 6:16-19 makes it crystal clear that God hates sin.

Still cradling their pain, brokenness and uncertainty, workshop participants are taken through this exploration of God's heart and character and brought to a place of realising that, far from being the unconcerned author of evil and injustice, God is undeniably full of compassion. He grieves with us when we suffer; He shares our pain and feels it as intensely as we do (Isaiah 63:9). When your pain weighs on you with the immediacy and ferocity of a gaping wound, this is a profound truth to grasp. But is it enough that God suffers alongside us? Thankfully, this is not the end of the story.

God may have given us free will, and chosen not to interfere with that freedom as and when it suits Him, but He is also all-powerful, and the wonderful out-working of this is that He alone has the power to turn a terrible loss into an immeasurable gain: He can bring good out of tragedy and wholeness out of utter brokenness. At this point, the workshops encourage participants to reflect on the ways in which God can redeem their personal suffering. To even ask this question takes monumental faith, and it is only possible through such a patient and carefully structured journey of reflection and revelation: fully acknowledging the depths of suffering and depravity that people have experienced; giving voice to doubts, questions and accusations against God that may have been buried out of shame, and recognising these as understandable responses, and; unlocking the key fundamental truths that God is good, just and full of compassion, and that Jesus' death has made it possible for our suffering to be fully redeemed. It is through the lens of these truths that participants are encouraged to invite God into their personal suffering so that He can start to redeem it on an intimate and individual heart level.

Now that participants are in a position to consider God as a loving Father, perhaps for the first time, this gives an opportunity for reflection on God's model for family. This is a crucial part of the healing process as many people in Rwanda (and all over the world) are living with the repercussions of a poor experience of family, and of fathers in particular. This can block people from being able to approach God in this way and fully experience the healing of the Father's heart, and these wounds and brokenness are often passed down through generations. Many of those who experienced the Rwandan genocide would also argue that those who grew up without a positive experience of parental love were much more likely to turn violently against their neighbour. The healing and reconciliation workshops must therefore address this stumbling block and include a time of ministry that is specifically about experiencing the Father's love. Again, this is only possible, only imaginable, on the basis of what participants have experienced in the earlier sessions, but the conviction of the HWEC teaching is that restoration and reconciliation begins at home, with families: before countries can be united, families must be healed.

BUILDING THE WALLS

As participants start to glimpse the unthinkable possibility of true healing, freedom from pain, and authentic reconciliation, it is tempting to rush on towards this promise. However, they are encouraged to pause in this place for a moment and to fully dwell on their wounds and loss, to face their pain head on and express all that has been taken from them. This will be the firm structure that will support and reinforce genuine and lasting reconciliation. Hearing each other's stories, sharing in each other's pain and praying together, regardless of ethnic differences, is a powerful healing tool.

John 10:10 is a particularly central passage for the healing workshops, where Jesus tells us that, "The thief comes only to steal and kill and destroy; I have come that they might have life and have it to the full." Here, we see the disconnection between our real-life experiences and what God truly intends for us. Having begun by considering God's original intention for human relationships, and for unity in diversity, workshop participants start to see the ways in which Satan, the thief, has robbed them – as individuals, as families, as ethnic groups, and as nations. Tangible and material losses are the easiest to identify, including family members, homes and possessions, but ethnic conflict also robs people of many precious inner qualities and certainties that are harder to pin down. These might include love, trust, dignity, a sense of peace and security, hope for the future, self-esteem or self-belief. As participants start to consider what they, themselves, have lost, this session also brings to light the fact that no-one comes out of ethnic conflict intact: every individual and every ethnic group is robbed on some level, and many of these losses are common to both sides of the divide. This process can be eye-opening as participants start to see their own sense of loss and brokenness from a wider perspective, without diminishing personal loss and suffering. Acknowledging our losses – individually and collectively – also helps us to recognise the false beliefs that have grown out of the conflict and taken root in our hearts: beliefs about God, about ourselves, and about those around us. One of the main things that the thief tries to rob is truth; in fact, Jesus calls him the "father of lies" (John 8:44). Satan delights when we believe his lies, and when we lose faith in God and in our fellow human beings.

This understanding of Satan as the "the thief" is not about shifting the blame so that no-one has to take responsibility for their own choices; we have seen that God gave us free will, and therefore we are responsible for how we behave and how we relate to those around us. Rather, the aim of this session is to recognise that the thief's goal is to rob us – all of us – of the true character of God. If every individual, every family, every community, and every nation is not released into its full identity and restored to its full potential, according to God's character and His intended plan, then we are all at a loss.

The thief therefore leaves us all deeply wounded and in need of healing. The good news is that God feels our pain, takes our wounds seriously, and promises to restore us (Jeremiah 30:17). This part of the workshop helps participants to understand what it means to continue to live out of a wounded spirit, and a wounded identity, and sombrely explores the potential, and very real, dangers of a life lived in this way. Unhealed wounds are like a poison that starts to take over the whole body, and that is why we so often see devastating cycles of conflict, where those that were once oppressed rise up and act violently or unjustly out of their wounded spirits.

David was eight years old when he lost his father during the genocide, and 28 when he attended the HWEC workshops as part of a choir of young people. He therefore has many painful years of personal experience that testify to the dangers of not addressing this loss, and this pain, on a deep level:

> It is like saying to people, "Just calm down. You lost something, you lost your relative, but calm down. Don't think about it. He's dead. He's passed away. You will never see him again. Just calm down. Just continue, continue." But teenagers started to realise that we had really lost someone, as happened to me: I realised that my dad had passed away. In 1997-1998, I started struggling. And this is the same case. 15 years or 100 years later, this problem can come back: "You killed us in 1994! We are in 2020 and we have to kill you back, because it is our turn to kill you!"

When his sister married a Hutu man, David refused to attend the wedding or to accept the marriage, because he was still living from such a wounded spirit. He was still carrying the pain and loss of all that had been taken from him, and this translated into anger, hatred, mistrust, and a desire for revenge. It was only after God healed and renewed his heart and mind through the transformative experience of the HWEC workshops that he came to deeply regret this decision:

> From that time, I realised that I was wrong. I cried a lot because I thought: "I didn't go to my sister's wedding because of that hatred." But I did something that was a significant sign. In our culture, a brother gives his sister to a man to be married, so during the wedding I was supposed to give my sister to her husband, but I was not there. I don't know what happened on the day. But even though the wedding had already happened, even though they are already husband and wife, I took the initiative to give my sister to her husband as a sign that I am participating in the wedding, even though it has already happened. When I realised that I was wrong, I did that: we took hands, and gave her to her husband, as a sign, and to finally fulfil my role. From that moment I can truly say that I am free.

The HWEC material gives the opportunity for participants to personally reflect on the ways in which we might be living out of a wounded spirit and believing lies about ourselves – our own value, worth, guilt or shame – about other ethnic groups, and about God. Crucially, participants are encouraged to fully express their emotions, openly and honestly, while acknowledging that this may feel deeply uncomfortable and counter-cultural. Odette describes the burden of guilt that she carried in her heart, and the powerful sense of release as she began to express it for the first time:

> The main problem I had was that I felt guilty, because when my children and I departed, I told the firstborn: "Take the kids! Take your sisters, take your sisters!" So that image of sending her away with the other children had stayed in me…that guilt of sending away my children, and then afterwards finding out how they were killed. It

> was that issue that was swollen in my heart when I met Rhiannon. So I closed my heart to the messages they were giving us. But the person who got to work inside my heart was Pastor Joseph Mugasa. Because, whenever we would meet, he would sing for me, and I just felt a bit released. So I opened my heart and started to express that anger and bitterness, and that guilt, and started to receive the message.

There are many reasons why we might prefer to keep our pain and raw emotions buried, and to "put on a brave face": shame, pride, mistrust, fear of opening up wounds that might never heal, fear of vulnerability, or a sense that our true feelings are not valid or acceptable. But, as we have seen, such pain can never stay truly buried; it grows and festers and starts to seep out into our beliefs, attitudes, relationships, words and actions. It becomes a defining part of our future, whether we want it to or not. The only way to reach authentic healing and freedom, and to avoid the dangerous consequences of unresolved conflict, is to overcome this resistance and to pass through our pain, anger or bitterness. Healing, forgiveness and reconciliation are not easily won.

This, then, is the very heart of the HWEC journey. This is the point where we are introduced to the ground-breaking discovery of Jesus as both the bearer of our sins and the bearer of our pain. Jesus has already paid the greatest and most agonising price for forgiveness and reconciliation, on our behalf. It is not only our sins and failures that are nailed to the cross, but also our grief and our sorrows: "Surely he took up our pain and bore our suffering…" (Isaiah 53:4). Most of us are familiar with the idea that we can take our sins to the cross and find forgiveness, because of the redemptive work of Jesus, but the claim that we can also bring our pain and heartbreak to the cross, and have this burden fully lifted, often comes as a revelation. The cross not only covers sin, but all of the consequences of sin in our world; in other words, Jesus not only takes responsibility for every sinful act, but also offers to hurt in our place. Devota beautifully articulates what this discovery meant to her:

> The first thing that touched my heart in the workshop was the topic about how God is able to receive our pain. I didn't know where to take my pain; I couldn't find a place to take it.

When people experience pain on such a monumental scale, it can feel like there is nothing to do but to bury it. Who or what could possibly be big enough or strong enough to carry this burden? The answer to this question is found at the foot of the cross.

The Cross Workshop is an opportunity for participants to take up Jesus' invitation in a practical way by physically handing their woundedness and grief over to him. This has become a defining session of the HWEC workshops and has been carried out with groups of people – large or small – across the nation of Rwanda and in many different countries and continents. Each person is encouraged to write down their most painful sufferings and losses on a piece of paper, and then to share these with others in small mixed ethnic groups. This is a powerful culmination of the groundwork that has been laid in the earlier sessions, leading participants to a point where they can fully express their pain in writing, and give voice to it, listening to each other with compassion and trusting each other with those things that are hardest to share. At the beginning of the HWEC process, this unity and vulnerability within the context of ethnic diversity would have seemed unreachable, but as the foundations have gradually been established, it is now possible to build these walls. Of course it is, undeniably, still one of the most difficult and painful moments of the journey.

After sharing and praying together, everyone nails their paper to the cross, demonstrating that they are taking their pain to the cross and leaving it there. This symbolic act helps to begin the process of letting go and lifting the burden. The papers are then removed and burned, and flowers are placed in the ashes to represent the fact that God is able to redeem our suffering, to bring life out of death and beauty out of ashes: "The Spirit of the Sovereign Lord is on me, because the Lord has anointed me…to comfort all who mourn and provide for those who grieve in Zion – to bestow on them a crown of beauty instead of ashes, the oil of joy instead of mourning, and a garment of praise instead of a spirit of despair." (Isaiah 61:1-3).

This practical out-working has proven extremely effective for many people, putting a spiritual truth into practice and helping to ignite the healing process. Some have found salvation for the first time as they come to know Jesus as the bearer of both their sins and their pain, and many have also experienced miraculous physical healing as they handed their heavy burdens over to God. We may need to bring our wounds and burdens to the cross again and again, but this is a powerful beginning. As people of all ethnic groups reveal the roots of their woundedness and come together at the foot of the cross, this encourages compassion and oneness, and offers a renewed hope that God can bring something living and beautiful out of the ashes of tragedy.

PUTTING ON THE CEILING

Many of us resist the idea of forgiveness because of the sense that it somehow diminishes the loss or pain of the wrongs that have been committed, brushing them aside, forgetting, or suggesting that they don't matter anymore. That is why it is so important that forgiveness comes only after people have had a chance to fully face and express their pain, and the devastating impact of someone else's wrong choices on their life. True and lasting forgiveness can only come out of a healed heart: if we try to forgive while still holding tightly to our pain and anger, the intensity of our woundedness will always win out in the end.

The cross shows us, vividly, that forgiveness is costly, but this must be weighed against the cost of unforgiveness. In the Lord's Prayer, we ask God to: "Forgive us our sins, for we also forgive everyone who sins against us" (Luke 11:4). We all need God's gracious gift of forgiveness, and if we withhold this from others, we are blocked from receiving it ourselves. Unforgiveness is also a burden in itself, and holds us back from knowing true freedom; again, we call to mind the thief who delights in robbing us from life in all its fullness. The Cross Workshop allows participants to pour their pain and suffering out onto Jesus, and therefore frees their hearts from those things that are keeping the door of forgiveness firmly closed. Gaudence describes the feeling of release from the burden of loss and anger, and the weariness of unforgiveness:

> When we arrived at the Cross Workshop, we held each other's hands, and it was time for the part of the workshop when you write all your pain and wounds down and you burn them. When we reached that point, I cried so much, because it was very touching for me. I was together with a person called Japheth. We were in the same choir, but I hated him so much because he was a Tutsi. At that time, I went and embraced him, saying, "I used to hate you because of who you were, but now I feel that I forgive you." After reconciling with him, I felt something falling down, falling off my heart, and I felt released.

As we realise how much we need God's free and gracious forgiveness in our own lives, we find ourselves more able and willing to extend this undeserved gift to the one who has wronged us. If we understand Jesus as the bearer of our sins, so that we can be judged as holy and pure, this must mean that he also takes responsibility for sins that have been committed against us. If we no longer count ourselves as guilty, how can we judge others, however atrocious their crimes? In forgiving, we are not denying the scale of the sins committed against us, but we are choosing to lay down our right to take revenge and trusting that those who are unrepentant will be judged by God.

So forgiveness may be a one-sided process, but reconciliation is only possible where there is repentance. At this stage in the workshops, participants are encouraged to ask themselves what they may need to repent of, personally, to God and to their neighbour. This session unpacks the full meaning and the transformational power of repentance, and shows us that we all need to examine ourselves for areas where repentance might be necessary. True repentance is a change of heart and mind that is reflected in a change of behaviour. It involves taking responsibility for the things we have done wrong, facing the consequences, and making restitution where possible. This kind of repentance is freeing and life-giving for everyone involved: the wrongdoer, the victim, and the wider community. It starts with peace and reconciliation with God, but it can also help the victim to forgive and can, incredibly, lead to restored relationships. The offender is released from the burden of guilt and shame, and the victim finds freedom from anger and bitterness. On a community level, repentance contributes to the process of justice, and brings a greater sense of peace and security. Ultimately, of course, the promise of repentance is that it opens the way for eternal life. Even if the victim still feels unable to forgive, the guilty party's repentance is recognised by God and He forgives in His infinite mercy and grace.

As an active participator in the genocide, Elia describes his journey of repentance while in prison for his crimes:

> In those days, I could not find peace. Wherever I would sit, I would not find peace. I remember, it was about 3pm, and I heard a voice, asking me: "Why did you have to kill those people? What did they do to you?" And I couldn't find the answer because I was not even able to see the one who was asking me. But what followed was just cries: just tears, many tears. At some point, I just cried out and started repenting, asking God for forgiveness. Telling God: "Just forgive me, because I did wrong to you." From that point, I made a decision that if anyone should ask me about what I have done or what I have witnessed, I would just tell them my story without beating around the bush… After they announced to me that I would be released, it troubled me, because I was wondering: "How am I going to face this society? The same people that I have wronged?" God is amazing. He knows how to turn bad into good.

For Elia, the need for repentance confronted him daily, burning and intense, and he couldn't ignore it. He had committed sinful acts with tangible consequences, and his sins were recognised by the state as crimes that could be categorised. For others, though, the HWEC workshops start to reveal their need for repentance and forgiveness more subtly, so that it gradually takes shape in their heart as a quiet conviction. This was the case for David: after his father was killed by some Hutus in the horrors of 1994, it took many years and a lot of ministry for him to realise that he, too, might need to repent and ask for forgiveness because of the attitude of his heart and mind:

> When I went to the healing and reconciliation sessions with Mercy Ministries, that is when I started to realise that I was wrong… After one week I started to think, within me, that I had to ask for forgiveness from the right person: my sister's husband. I think it was one day before we ended the workshop, we had a session about asking for forgiveness. Some people were Hutu and they asked for forgiveness for the things they had done wrong… Someone told me: "Someone who's Tutsi can come and hug me, and that will be a sign that I am forgiven by Tutsis." So I did that, but afterwards I realised that I still didn't like them. I was hugging him because I felt obliged to do that because I'm Tutsi, but I didn't love him really… After that, my heart started to tell me, "Because you hate them, you also have to ask for forgiveness." And I was 100% convinced that I had to tell my sister's husband; I had to say that I had hated him too much. I called him, asking him for forgiveness. He was the one I really hated because he took my sister, and it seemed to me that he didn't have to take her. This is where the hating came from. But even the other Hutus, I could not pretend that I really felt love for them in my heart. So I asked for forgiveness, because of the Mercy Ministries workshop. I even told Joseph: "Your ministry made me appreciate the cross." This was the only sin I could not speak about, or show to people. It was inside my heart. So I asked for forgiveness, and I have been forgiven. Glory to the Lord!

In this place of repentance and forgiveness, the workshops encourage people to "stand in the gap" and repent on behalf of whichever group they represent. This principle is based on God's words in Ezekiel 22:30, and on our mandate as a "royal priesthood" (1 Peter 2:9). In the Old Testament, we see that a key part of a priest's role was to bear the sins of the people before God, to identify with them, represent them and repent of sins on their behalf. Jesus is our greatest example of this, and this verse in 1 Peter reminds us that we are called to do the same. Indeed, for those who have attended the workshops feeling deeply wounded, angry, bitter and resistant, this has proven to be a hugely effective tool in softening hearts and releasing grace for forgiveness. Many of those who were so grievously wronged during the genocide will never be able to look their offender in the eye and hear a personal confession; either because the offender is unrepentant, or has since died, or because the atrocities were committed by an entire group and no-one will put their hand up to accept personal responsibility. Yet there are countless testimonies from the HWEC workshops of people who have found healing and the capacity to forgive through the powerful act of hearing someone confess and repent on behalf of their nation, their ethnic group, their community or their neighbours.

Elia describes how he reached this point in the workshops, and the profound impact his confession had on many Tutsi participants from his local community:

> One day, the African Evangelistic Enterprise organised a seminar… in our province, just nearby here. I was invited, and I was blessed to see that those people I had hurt were also invited. There were about 72 of us. The seminar started – the first day, the second day – but as they were teaching us, it felt like they were taking a long time. I started feeling like I was bursting. I wanted them to give me a chance to get out what was filling me. Then they taught us a lesson called, "To stand in the gap."… I started confessing right away. I apologised for my people, my tribe, who are still in denial. I can say that the journey of confessing and reconciliation started at that time, at that seminar. The place became small because they were just standing up and hugging me, and another one was taking my arm, because there were so many wanting to hug me. I felt released, like a burden lifted off me, and the cloud of fear and mistrust was just gone.

FINALLY, THE ROOF!

Only now can we crown this process of revelation, healing, forgiveness and repentance with the incredible possibility of genuine reconciliation, on both a personal and a collective level. The workshops end by returning to the idea of the Holy Nation, where everyone has equal value and all are welcome at the table. Odette describes the powerful impact of this symbolic feast:

> When I arrived and I saw the table prepared, and when I saw Pastor Joseph standing together with Rhiannon and Anastase, I just burst: I started crying and shouting, and making such a mess. Then the pastor told us that someone from a different ethnic group should try to comfort me, and then that person came, and he was putting sweets in my mouth, hugging me, and just trying to comfort me. I can say that that was the beginning of the journey of healing, the beginning of the healing process. What happened is that I started receiving inner peace, and I even started to see that forgiving is possible.

In a complete turnaround, prejudice and mistrust are replaced by affirmation and blessings. Again, this is part of our responsibility as a "royal priesthood": Deuteronomy 10:8 tells us that it was the role of the priests to pronounce blessings, with the authority of God. Blessing might involve affirming each other, sharing what we value about another person, group or culture, or speaking prophetic words over one another. Finally, diversity becomes something to celebrate and enjoy!

Once the Church is healed in this way, she can take her rightful place as the agent of healing and reconciliation in the community. In fact, this has started to happen as a natural overflow: many of those who have found new life, freedom and hope in a revelation of God's heart through the HWEC ministry have felt compelled to share the message and material of the workshops with their families and communities, and even further afield. Gaudence took the message first to her mother:

> I committed myself to go and teach my mum about what I had taken away from the workshop. Before this, every time I was reminded that my father was in prison, I would throw down everything that I had in my hand and say: "Oh, this is typical Tutsi!" But after the workshop, I committed to go and testify to my mother and to tell her what had happened to me. Because she, also, would relate every pain that she had in that time to the Tutsi. She would say: "All this is because of the Tutsi." Later, my mother was also released, and now she is ok.

Later, she felt a calling from God to reach out to people outside of her own family and community who also desperately needed to receive this ministry:

> In that time, they were planning for a workshop in a northern province. It's a place called Byumba. They were planning a workshop there, and I didn't know much about the people who would go there, but I heard a voice telling me to be prepared, and that I would be among the people who would go.

After God so dramatically redeemed her own suffering, Odette also realised that her local community needed to hear the message of HWEC and receive God's healing:

> I took those people of God to take the message to my home town. When we got there, and my former neighbours saw that I was coming with those people, they wanted to run. They thought I was coming to have them cursed or something. But finally, they came and they sat with us. The people of God ministered to them the message of HWEC, and what God did in my home town was amazing! People started confessing, and survivors forgave... It was such a big story of healing and reconciliation.

The thief may have come to steal and to destroy, but as more and more people are coming together at the foot of the cross and rising up from that place as new creations, all that was lost is truly being restored, in Rwanda and beyond.

A last word here must go to Devota:

> I'm so happy. From all the bad things that I went through, God has redeemed that pain into something good, and now I have hope for the future. Amen!

If God can do this for a woman who saw both of her children brutally and mercilessly murdered, who was herself savagely wounded and burned alive in her home, and who spent almost two months lying alone in a forest, waiting for death, what then is impossible for Him?

CHAPTER THREE

The Fullness of Forgiveness

The voices of those who have passed through the HWEC workshops tell some truly miraculous stories of healing, forgiveness and reconciliation that have taken place in Rwanda over the last 20 years, and God's incredible restoration of relationships, finances, attitudes, and hope. Christophe Mbonyingabo, founder of CARSA, testifies to the power of forgiveness to bring new life, and to have the last word over evil and darkness:

> We have seen that forgiveness, including repentance, is the key to real transformation of lives affected by conflict. People who cannot forgive are often stuck in various areas of their lives, most of the time not only emotionally but economically and socially as well. True forgiveness, however, sets free and opens the life in abundance that God intended for us human beings. Forgiveness brings blessings to our lives and very often this includes economic growth, restoration of relationships and advance in development. The power of God can change situations and redeem suffering. Forgiveness has huge power over evil and can overcome any evil deed.

We have heard the amazing transformation that took place in David's life, and the power this held for his family, community and colleagues, and thankfully his is just one of many testimonies of how God can utterly redeem lives, relationships and situations through the tangible power of forgiveness.

Following an excruciating testimony, Odette tells the outrageously redemptive story of her first encounter with the man who handed her children over to the militia to be slowly and brutally murdered in the most unthinkable ways. After the genocide, she had taken in many orphans, and the church provided her with a job in a local shop to help her to support so many children:

> Before [the workshop], I would not receive any customer from the Hutu tribe, because I was so mad at them; I hated them wholeheartedly. When that person came back into the country, he came to the shop. He did not know that I was the one working there, so when he found me he wanted to run. He was afraid, and he started shaking. So, I told him, "No, no, no. I have forgiven you. I have released you. I received messages which helped me to release you in my heart." We sat down and he told me the whole story: how my children were killed, how he abandoned them. He told me the whole journey of my children being killed. We started to cry together, and as I was crying I felt a big, heavy burden being lifted off me, piece by piece. I was crying, and as my tears were coming out of me, I felt that they were bringing out some of the stuff that was in my heart.

Having experienced the pain of seeing her father put in prison, and the bitterness that started to take hold of her and her mother, Gaudence experienced God's redemption of her suffering when He instructed a Tutsi pastor to stand in the place of her father. She speaks of a profound restoration of family, love and genuine joy:

> I experienced how much God redeemed this horror. Because at that time I was single, and the time came for me to get married, and that family [the Tutsi pastor and his wife] were like my real father and mother. I remember how the mother took care of me, sending me

> messages: "How are you doing?" Helping me. They are the ones who were responsible for every part of my wedding ceremony, everything. That was my family. I experienced love there, and I really felt how God redeemed my sorrow. I realised that it's only at the cross that people of different ethnic groups can meet and become one, and from that time I just committed myself to be the one who gives that message of healing and reconciliation. I want to testify to the other Rwandese that it is God who really redeems our pain and sorrow.

Omer's description of meeting, dating and marrying his wife is a true testament to the lengths that God can go to in order to renew our minds and restore relationships, one by one:

> I thought: "Why am I loving a Tutsi? And what is attracting me to that Tutsi?"... It took me two and a half years to give in to my wish to marry her. During that time, I was asking myself: "Am I serious? Am I able to live with someone to whom we did a wrong thing? Hutus killed her father, her mum, her brothers and sisters. Will I cope with the mourning period, when she is suffering, she is remembering?" I tried to love other girls, and thought: "Maybe I can love someone else." But it didn't happen. So I found that, maybe, I am serious. I can manage it.
>
> I asked her to marry me and, after a few months, she responded positively, and now we have two children, and we work together here... We have crises as others have crises, and we enjoy each other. We have a life like everyone else. There is nothing visible that is connected to ethnicity, to my background, or to her background. The history of Rwanda doesn't affect us in a negative way. When there is something wrong – maybe some political issue which is connected to the background of Rwanda, either on the Hutu side or the Tutsi side – we are not affected. We judge it as people who are healed, as people of the Holy Nation, as people who are Christian.

Maybe, just maybe, this relationship between husband and wife is a beautiful glimpse into the future for Rwanda as a whole.

As we have seen, it is not just the victims of the genocide that are in desperate need of God's healing. When it comes to conflict and atrocities of this scale, no-one emerges whole and unscathed. Elia's story is testament to this. Here, he describes his role in the genocide with raw honesty and deep conviction:

> I am one of the criminals who perpetrated the genocide. I take the responsibility, I do not blame others, because no-one influenced me: it was my heart that did it… I was looking after my father's cows. When we would meet other Tutsis in that field, we would beat them and mistreat them. When '94 came, we did not hold back, we just entered the killings, and I killed; I mean, I really killed people.

In prison, he was brought to the depths of despair and shame about what he had done to his Tutsi neighbours, and he cried out in repentance and asked God for forgiveness. Unbelievably, when he was released and returned to his community, he was greeted with life-giving grace:

> The first friends that I met were the same people whose family I had killed. It was not false, or just a smile to cover up something hidden inside; those friends were my neighbours. My brother knows them and has met them. I really took a major role in killing their siblings, but God just connected us and now we are a team, healing the hearts of Rwandans. One thing is amazing: I had a wedding. Before the genocide, I had taken a wife but in an illegal way. But after I got saved, I had to legalise my marriage, so we got married legally. What is amazing is that the bridesmaids were the same people, the victims, whose family I had killed. Now we are living peacefully with them. When I need money, I can go and borrow from them. When they need money, I can give it to them when I have it. If I need a bicycle to use, then they have it. And if I have it, and they need it, I just lend it to them.

There is nothing in our language or human experience that can explain forgiveness of this magnitude, of neighbours living alongside each other after such brutal, wholehearted betrayal. Many will (and do) find this kind of forgiveness offensive, which is why the HWEC workshop material spends a lot of time on the concept of forgiveness, concluding that it is as much about releasing ourselves and enabling us to move forward with our lives as it is about extending grace towards the person who has wronged us. After experiencing the power of forgiveness for herself, Gaudence committed to taking the message of healing and reconciliation to others, and she describes the process of guiding people towards forgiveness:

> We don't force him or her to forgive, because I know that it is not easy to forgive, and forgiveness is a process. It is not the kind of thing that you can just do immediately. But what we do…is to show him how painful it is not to forgive, how you are tied to the other person. It is like you are together with the person who offended you. And we tell him how it can also bring death, because of that pain. We don't focus on telling him to forgive but we show him how painful it is to remain with that kind of pain, and we tell him that it is a process. After a time, when people realise that it is real, that it is true, they forgive. They commit themselves to forgive, without being forced.

Like Gaudence, many of the first workshop participants have gone on to take the HWEC material to their families, communities, and further afield. Devota lives and works in Kigali, spending much of her time teaching the word of God, and she finds that out of her own long, drawn out and near fatal ordeal she is uniquely positioned to reach and connect with some of the women in her congregation who have lost all sense of trust in anyone else:

> Those people who are wounded, they are in our churches, and I am very sensitive to those people. I can look at them and recognise them because I also lived in that situation. I just find a strategy, an approach, that I can use to reach that person. And bit by bit, I reach her, and we have a conversation.

What is clear is that the experience of forgiveness is so powerful that it cannot be contained, and it overflows. But it is also deeply personal, so that the particular nature and course of this overflow is shaped by the individual. Knowing His children, knowing what they have endured – even having endured it with them – God works out of the uniqueness of each healed heart.

ODETTE'S MINISTRY

Odette, who lost her husband, three children and mother in the genocide, felt a personal calling to organise a HWEC workshop for other widows. These were women who were suffering in every way imaginable: some had visible cuts and wounds from machetes, others had contracted HIV or become pregnant as a result of rape, many were lost and hopeless – one way or another, all were deeply scarred. In Odette's words: "We were dead. Many could not even leave their houses, full of hopelessness."

The widows were initially sceptical of Odette, thinking that she must have been manipulated by Hutus, but God worked in them to change their hearts towards her. She set up a weekly prayer meeting for the women, but she also knew that there was an urgent practical need that had to be met. Having lost their husbands and many – if not all – of their family members, the women were left to care and provide for themselves, yet many of them were too injured, sick or weak to work. Odette therefore led a small regional team that would visit each woman in her own home, and contribute to her material needs as much as possible – whether it be rebuilding houses, providing food, or helping with school fees and resources for her children. The women are also now in a position to form a collective, where they work together to seek out income-generating initiatives, such as raising chickens or pigs on their land.

But it is not only the widows of men who were killed in the genocide that have been left with nothing and no-one. Odette also works with Hutu women whose husbands have been sentenced to prison or community work. Incredibly, Odette's heart is for these two groups of women to come together, and to support and collaborate with each other. These amazing women could be a symbol of all that is possible when we meet on the common ground of pain and loss and are united in our desire for a hope and a future.

Not content to stop there, Odette has also brought together a group 16-22 year-olds whose parents were either victims of the genocide, or imprisoned for the part they played. Using her training as a HWEC facilitator, she listened to these young people's heartbreaking stories and guided them through the different stages of the workshop. It ended with Odette, herself, standing in the gap on behalf of their parents, asking for forgiveness for the suffering they have endured. Finally, as she sent these children off to continue their healing journeys, they were able to laugh together.

CLEMENTINE'S MINISTRY

Clementine was the daughter of a Hutu mother and a Tutsi father, and after her father died she was taught to bury her emotions and resign herself to a life of suffering. It was only through her own children's games and role play that God showed her that she was teaching them this same behaviour. She participated in a HWEC workshop in 2000, where she found healing and forgiveness, and the freedom to fully be herself and express her emotions. This transformed her heart, her marriage and her family. Later, she felt moved to join a regional team in Gitarama to facilitate HWEC workshops and help this transformational ministry to reach more people.

Above all, Clementine's heart is for children, and for the restoration of families, and she is able to reach people on this level because of her own family story. It has not been easy for her to share her personal trauma, but her vulnerability and courage have inspired others to open up and explore their own suffering. Sharing her own story provides a forum for others to do the same, inviting them to be real and honest, free from shame or judgment. She recalls a meeting in Nyamata, where she spoke about her family history with a group of women who had been widowed by the genocide. Through her own honesty and openness, Clementine had been able to create such an environment of trust and safety that many of the women began to pour out those things they had been guarding in their hearts. Some even admitted that they felt guilty claiming to be genocide survivors as they had lost their Tutsi husbands but were, themselves, Hutus. Others felt able to speak out, for the first time, about the fact that they had suffered abuse and even rape at the hands of rogue soldiers on both sides – not just the Interahamwe.

Word about the impact of Clementine's work with families reached the leader of the district and he asked her to speak to government officials at the end of the national family week. She spoke about the needs of children within the home, and the danger of leaving these needs unmet. She traced the trajectory of damaging consequences on our personal and professional lives, giving specific and practical examples and drawing on her own experience. For example, if a child learns from an early age that they have to rely on themselves to get what they need to survive, it is hardly surprising if that person ends up stealing and being dishonest in their work as an adult. Listening to Clementine speak, this hit home for the government leaders as they were only too aware of such dishonesty and corruption among administrators and authorities. Many stood and admitted that they were guilty of some of the very things Clementine had been talking about. Even now, some of these government leaders still call Clementine and ask for prayer, as they struggle with temptation to dishonesty and corruption in their influential positions.

Even when there was no longer any financial support for the Gitarama team, Clementine continued to press on and take every opportunity to spread the message of healing and transformation. She has become recognised and well-respected for her work with AEE and CARSA, and is often invited to speak at seminars and events around Gitarama, and further afield. The mayor of Gitarama regularly organises gatherings where the wives of government leaders are given space to talk about their pain and hear the message of healing, and Clementine raises funds to keep these activities going.

Working tirelessly since 2005, she has seen real, tangible change in relationships, homes, government institutions, and in the community as a whole:

> Through the genocide, trust had been vastly destroyed, but people are now trying to come together again. Before so many people had been reached with the message of healing and reconciliation, the community was deeply divided; especially during the commemoration of the genocide in the mourning week, when some would go to the memorial and others would not even leave their beds. Now, I see people coming together and getting involved in the events. Moreover, many families have been changed and children's broken hearts healed.

TRUTH, GRACE AND JUSTICE

The power of openness, honesty and dialogue in bringing about healing and reconciliation is perhaps most clearly depicted in the form of the Gacaca courts. These grassroots, community courts were one of the unique elements to emerge from the ashes of the genocide, taking "trial by a jury of your peers" to a whole new level. Due to the sheer number of Rwandans suspected of having taken part in the killings, the established justice system – both within Rwanda and on an international level – simply could not cope with the volume of prosecutions. Hundreds of thousands of genocide suspects were being held in crowded and festering jails, awaiting prosecution, and the number was rising. At crisis point, the Rwandan government implemented the Gacaca courts, where suspects were tried within their own communities. Lay judges were elected by their communities and trained in the necessary legal procedures, and the Gacaca were launched in June 2002.

This unprecedented judicial process posed both a challenge and an opportunity for AEE and the regional teams. The impact and the success of the courts inevitably varied from one community to the next as there was no blueprint or tried and tested structure to the proceedings. It was a dangerous gamble in some respects, as the raw nature of the courts brought out some explosive reactions on all sides. There was an urgent need to try and shape the process into something productive and healing, and the regional teams rose to this challenge. It wasn't a perfect process, but we could hardly expect more from a deeply hurting people trying desperately to heal.

Almost every adult Rwandan has participated in the Gacaca in one way or another, and both suspects and survivors often emphasise how transformative it was to be able to talk openly, with their friends and neighbours, about what exactly had taken place during those one hundred days. This extraordinary format created a space and structure for survivors to articulate their pain, to identify the perpetrators of their personal suffering, and to participate in the justice process as a community. For suspects, there was an opportunity to take ownership over their actions, to witness the consequences in the lives of survivors and victims' families, and to express remorse or repentance.

Perpetrators and victims, suspects and survivors often attach a lot of weight to the Gacaca as a key part of the healing process. On both sides, the opportunity and invitation to speak openly, rather than burying emotions and being consumed by anger or shame, opened the way for genuine healing. This intensely communal form of legal proceedings seems to have freed many people from the feelings of loneliness and isolation that can come with grief or shame. Survivors were able to publicly acknowledge their pain and share that burden with their friends and neighbours, and many perpetrators speak of feeling released from their fear of social exclusion once they had looked into the eyes of those they had most wounded, confessed and repented of their crimes. Gaudence describes the lasting impact this had on healing and unity within communities:

> For me, the good thing that I saw in Gacaca is when people would just sit down, and people were free to tell the whole truth. One person could rise and say, "I am the one who killed your family," before any person accused him or her. Those cases when people could

> just confess, without other people accusing him. It helped some people to be released, hearing a person confessing the bad things that he had done to them. Some people were released, and they forgave each other, and that was a good experience because it released people, it reconciled people. From that Gacaca court, many people – many Tutsi and Hutu – reconciled to the level that they can marry each other: Hutu can marry a Tutsi and Tutsi can marry a Hutu, because of that kind of justice, and the truth that they confessed.

Crucially, the Gacaca process demonstrates that repentance and forgiveness don't take the place of restitution. Rather, grace and justice were held in harmony as convicted perpetrators – including those who fully confessed and repented – were given varying sentences or were expected to carry out certain reparations for their actions, and the fulfilment of these sentences sows into the ongoing healing process. Elia describes how his own programme of reparations is built on a mutual respect and understanding between himself and the family of his victims – surely an inconceivable notion:

> The consequences cannot be avoided, because everyone who was in this country had to face the consequences, the challenges. Now there is this programme of paying back – restitution – to the victims of the genocide. So it has to have a consequence, financially, to the family. I'm working to pay them back. I am also struggling to take care of my family, so it's tricky… But the blessing I have is that we understand each other. We agree. I tell them: "This is my level, financially, so allow me to pay you back month by month." And they agree. To give you an example, there is a person to whom I owe 200,000 RF in total. But because of that unity, he just accepts whatever I have.

So when we talk about reconciliation, it is not about keeping quiet in order to live side by side, trying to act in a loving way because we think it is the right thing to do, while our hearts churn with anger and hatred. That is not living, and nor is it loving. Neither does forgiveness wipe the slate clean and take the place of repentance and reparation. The experience of the Rwandan people, borne out of necessity and desperation in the face of such unprecedented culpability, demonstrates that there is a way forward that holds grace, mercy and justice in the balance.

TRANSFORMING COMMUNITIES

It is in the powerful and deeply moving stories of personal healing, forgiveness and reconciliation – of victim forgiving perpetrator, and neighbour being reconciled to neighbour – that more far-reaching community transformation is born. It is tempting to immediately set about trying to rebuild communities in a practical way, and to repair those things that are physically and visibly damaged, but this would be a cosmetic patch-up that doesn't reach the roots of the problem. It is the brokenness that is hidden and buried, deeply cleaved in wounded hearts, that is desperately in need of healing, and it is healing on this level that fuels practical restoration.

The truth that is gradually rising to the surface is that diversity itself is not the problem. The real enemy is neither Hutu nor Tutsi, but rather the pressures and struggles that people (of all ethnic groups) face every day; including health, lifestyle and family issues, poverty, mistrust and suspicion. These are the adversaries that must be confronted in order to make the ground less fertile for the seeds of division, prejudice and hatred. Genuine and lasting community transformation can only come through dealing with these issues head-on, and educating younger generations, rather than hiding from what has gone before. This is the only way to secure the future of the nation of Rwanda, and to bolster communities against sliding backwards into the devastation of the past.

In collaboration with churches, local government leaders, other local NGOs, institutions and organisations, Rabagirana Ministries is empowering communities to take ownership of sustainable projects and initiatives, helping them to realise their God-given capacity to be their own solution to their problems. It is not a case of depending on "mzungu superheroes" – foreign aid, overseas voluntary workers and international NGOs – to pull people out of poverty, to temporarily provide relief, to ship in resources and build new homes. Community transformation needs to start with healed individuals, invigorated with hope for the future, and motivated by love for their neighbours. For communities and families that feel hopeless and helpless, the very fact that someone values them enough to sit with them and understand their struggles, believes in them to have the strength and the skills to find their own way forward, and is willing to work alongside them to do so, is life-giving.

Those who have experienced God's healing and reconciliation through the HWEC workshops testify that one of the most powerful fruits of the process is the transformation from hopelessness, brokenness and passive drifting, to a new and active hope for the future. Devota beautifully expresses this feeling of empowerment, and the motivation to do something practical and life-affirming:

> I couldn't enjoy life here. I was expecting to have full joy only in Heaven. I didn't have a desire to have a good life here. My daily prayer was just: "God, take me from this world." All the things I was doing to serve God were just a price that I would pay for God to take me out of this world… From the moment that I realised that Jesus is my pain-bearer, I felt released, and my hope – the hope of living – was brought back to me. I felt that I was alive, and I had hope for the future. And from that point on, I started to enjoy serving God.

So although the workshops initially focused on the wounds caused directly by the genocide, individual healing and reconciliation has become a springboard for practical peace-building in all areas of family and community life. Many of the people who have come through the HWEC workshops go on to take part in the Training of Facilitators, equipping them to take the message of the workshops back to their own communities, and they then set out to lead, influence, challenge and bless their communities in many different ways; from charitable outreach and education, to drama, music and dance. The limitless love, power and creativity of God are being poured out through the particular gifts and passions of individuals, and uniting teams around a common heart.

PEACE-BUILDING

The Impuhwe ("compassion") team works with communities in Rubavu, in the north of Rwanda, identifying the people who are most in need of compassion, healing and practical assistance to break free from poverty. One of the most powerful things they do is simply to sit with people, talk with them, and show them that they are valued and not forgotten. This gentle act of love and grace is deeply transformative for people, and invites vulnerability and openness. The team joins with them in their suffering, and they then journey together towards a solution. The work of Impuhwe notably extends to the Twa people, who have so often been marginalised or excluded, showing them that they are loved, valued and appreciated as integral to Rwandan society.

This is "Love your neighbour" in action, in the most real and raw way: people working together, day by day and side by side, to build a new stove, or even a new house for their neighbour, for no money and no reward, but simply because, having walked through the fire together, they believe in and hope for a better future.

The Impuhwe team helps people to identify the root cause of their current poverty, and supports them to put in place practical solutions. They have become invaluable advocates for the people of their communities, seeking out and speaking up for the "hidden" people who don't have a voice, or who can't bear the hope that there might be something better for them. It is through these on-the-ground advocates that the small Rabagirana team in Rubavu has been able to connect with those who most need their help, and join with Impuhwe to provide whatever materials, resources or support they can. For example, through careful negotiations with the local government, Jean-Paul and the team (MMI at the time) were able to reach an agreement whereby, if the community build new houses themselves, the government will provide the roofs. In a climate that moves seamlessly from beating sunshine to torrential rain, this is no small offering. Similarly, through the Impuhwe team's outreach amongst the Twa, MMI was able to provide clay for the many potters of that community, and they have now formed a co-operative with people of other ethnicities, working together to generate income. Out of diversity, unity and productivity are born. As one staff member puts it:

> That is our strength… That diversity is not a sin, it is not bad. Many people used to say, "To be Hutu, Twa, Tutsi, this is an evil thing." And we try to tell them, "It is not evil. It is evil because the devil tried to make it like that, to use it. But if you look deeply, you will see that it is a treasure."

Nowhere is this more true, and more urgent, than in the Church. There is a tendency for new churches to grow out of disagreement, conflict and rifts, and the Church in Rwanda as a whole needs to be healed and released from its failure during the genocide. More than ever, this must start from a place of unity. The "We Are One" group is made up of representatives from various denominations, who travel to different churches with drama and peace-building songs as a compelling, living and breathing symbol of what is possible.

YOUNG PEOPLE AS PEACE-BEARERS

A large part of what makes these groups and initiatives so ground-breaking and future-proof is that they involve so many young people who have truly taken the words of 1 Timothy to heart: "Don't let anyone look down on you because you are young, but set an example for the believers in speech, in conduct, in love, in faith and in purity." (4:12). Many of Rwanda's children and teenagers face the social, emotional and economic consequences of the genocide without any comprehensive understanding of what happened in their country back in 1994. There is still no agreed historical narrative that can be taught in schools, because the political emphasis is on unity, and there is resistance to anything that might threaten this veneer of peace and oneness. AEE worked hard to adapt the HWEC material for use in schools, and it is used by many teachers to help shape children's moral values, however it is still not recognised as part of the curriculum. Nevertheless, this work has helped teachers to become more aware of the needs of children, and to invest more in the pastoral care of their students.

Christian Action for Reconciliation and Social Assistance (CARSA) was founded in 2002, with the goal of promoting reconciliation, reconstruction and consolidation of a peaceful society, and they particularly saw the need to reach students at secondary school and university. Up until this point, there had been no specific ministry for these young people, so AEE was keen to support CARSA. In partnership with movements such as Groupe Biblique Universitaire (GBU) and Communauté Étudiants Pentecôtistes (CEP), MMI ran workshops for students all over the country: between 2006 and 2011, around 2,160 students and 320 teachers attended HWEC workshops. A further 5,870 students and 467 teachers were reached with the message of healing and reconciliation through conferences, but did not personally pass through the healing process.

Since then, young people within the universities have taken the initiative to form their own teams and run workshops, as they have seen the benefit in their own lives and communities, and recognise this as a bedrock for the future of Rwandan society. The two main Christian student organisations, GBU and ONAP (Organization Nationale des Academiciens Pentecôtistes) have made it a priority to take all new Christian university students through the workshops, and to train new facilitators as they go, so that the movement is owned and sustained by the students themselves, in every university. One student group was even given a platform to lead commemoration events during the national mourning period, allowing young people to lead the way in promoting healing, peace and hope for the nation.

More recently, CARSA's focus has shifted to those children and young people who were born into post-genocide Rwanda. The vision is to empower them to become peace-builders in society by teaching them not only how to deal with the consequences of conflict, but how to manage conflict in positive ways. Similarly, when asked about the messages that young people need to receive from their parents, teachers and elders in the community, Omer of MMI responded:

> We teach them that, even if they're not accepted officially, our differences are our means to develop, to grow, to build our country. Because our differences are based, not on hatred or division, but on things which are good.

Indeed, Rabagirana is seeing many young people grasp the importance of confronting the history of their country and communities, and taking up the mantle of building a better future. After attending youth camps, and passing through the Community Development training (originally developed by Renée Schudel of Le Rucher Geneva), many have been inspired to use their individual creative gifts to build peace and transformation into their communities, and to leave a legacy for generations to come. They partner with local government leaders to identify the need in the community, and opportunities to contribute to the welfare of others, and then divide into smaller working groups, according to their individual skills. These are practical and active groups, engaged in projects such as building more economical stoves for widows of the genocide, installing toilets for genocide survivors, repairing the roads and painting their own classrooms. In these simple, straightforward ways, they are sending a message to their peers, and to the community as a whole: "We have the power and the responsibility to make a difference to each other, and to rebuild and uplift this community. If not us, then who?"

Urumuri ("light") is a group of young people who communicate the message of peace-building through drama, acting out scenarios relating to reconciliation, but also broader family and lifestyle issues, such as domestic abuse, drug and alcohol addiction, and health. By making these struggles visible, acknowledging and exploring them, they are helping to break the power of shame and silence, and highlight ways of confronting and dealing with them. They work with the local government to identify public opportunities to present their message, and have had the chance to perform at open events, in front of the whole community, as well as district officials. Trips to memorial sites, such as the Gisozi memorial, give them a more rounded view and deeper understanding of the genocide, so that they are able to act powerfully from the heart.

One of many beautiful success stories amongst young people in Rubavu is that of a dance group, consisting of many street boys who had dropped out of school. Members of Impuhwe drew alongside these boys, and as they built up a relationship with them they began to understand their reasons for leaving school. For the most part, these were rooted in the daily struggle of living in poverty, as well as lack of adequate care from parents. Stories like that of Aphrodis are all too common: when Elianne of Impuhwe first met him, he was carrying around a lot of anger towards his father, who had abandoned the family and left them in such desperate conditions. Aphrodis and his mother and young siblings were living in a shack the size of a small shed, but far less weather-proof and suitable for habitation, so that when it rained (Rwanda-style, for days and weeks at a time) they would have to huddle in one corner to try and stay dry. Young as he was, he dropped out of school as he felt the burden of needing to work to support his mother and younger siblings.

Elianne realised that Aphrodis, and many of the other boys, were talented at traditional dancing, and that it seemed to make them come alive and lift them out of their anger and hopelessness, even just for a moment. She encouraged them to get together as a dance group and focus their energy on something positive and proactive, rather than just roaming the streets. The group now performs for people at various events, usually following a HWEC workshop, to convey the message of healing, reconciliation and peace-building through lively, impassioned dance. They are a vibrant embodiment of the release of joy that people have experienced when they have allowed God to heal and restore their wounded hearts. The dancers share the money they are paid for such performances, and can then use it to support their families. Aphrodis doesn't even spare the change to buy himself a drink after a show; every penny he earns goes straight to his mother.

Through MMI, Elianne was also able to source books and pens for the boys, and encourage them about the importance of school as an investment in their future, building strong foundations and giving them a way forward, a way out of their current situations. MMI staff in Rubavu arranged for traditional costumes for the dancers, so that they look the part of a professional dance troupe and can secure more bookings: bright red, orange and green tunics, with sashes across the chest, and impressive, thick headdresses of dried grasses. Finally, the team sourced some plastic sheeting to cover the roof of Aphrodis' family home, so that they might get some relief from the elements. More recently, members of the community, led by Elianne, her husband and the dancers, have completed the building of a new house for this family.

Through the love, attention and perseverance of Elianne and Impuhwe, and their advocacy with MMI (and now Rabagirana), these boys have found community, value and purpose, and they in turn powerfully communicate messages of reconciliation, peace and hope to many others through their talents. Elianne showed Aphrodis that he had the power to take responsibility and do something proactive to provide for his family, with real, tangible results. Now, his face shines when he dances.

The "Peacemakers" group also focuses on these young people who are suffering the after-shocks of genocide, whether they are aware of it or not. The group goes into schools to share dialogue and testimonies, and specifically tries to identify those children who are orphaned, desperately poor, or living in loneliness. Again, they get to know these young people, talk and share with them, allow them to acknowledge and express how they are feeling, without fear or shame, and encourage them that there is hope for tomorrow.

Working with young people, and reaching them where they are, is the greatest investment in the future of Rwanda. In collaboration with local leaders, MMI established its own courses to equip young people with practical skills and vocational training. Many of the youth have not been to school, or were not able to finish their studies, so this is an opportunity to be trained in skills that they can then put to use to benefit their families and communities. As young people are healed, equipped, empowered and sent out, God is using them to set an example, and to lay firm foundations for the future of this nation.

COMMUNITY DEVELOPMENT INITIATIVES

Community development is everyone's responsibility, but there is a particular calling on the Church and local government leaders to be forward-thinking and motivated in identifying the prevailing problems, and mobilising local people to implement solutions. Representatives from MMI (and now Rabagirana) meet first of all with these local leaders and explore ways in which they can work together towards practical solutions for lasting transformation. Leaders from each district are given a forum to sit together and assess the social and environmental needs in their area, encompassing poverty, education, health, gender and spirituality. Advocates within the local community are able to bring particular families or situations to the attention of Jean-Paul and the team, as well as providing on-the-ground evaluation of the success of various projects.

Rubavu has been a key area for community outreach, and delegates from Rabagirana's annual International School of Reconciliation travel to the area for three days of working alongside the community on projects or initiatives. This might involve helping to build a kitchen or toilet for a genocide survivor, planting trees, or teaching local families about hygiene and sanitation. These three days, in particular, are a wonderful expression of unity in diversity, and an affirmation to the people of Rwanda that they are no longer forgotten, and their suffering is no longer overlooked. Representatives from all over the world attend ISOR, and when they enter a rural community in Rubavu, ready to get their hands dirty and give their time and energy for one person, one family or one community, that sends a strong and transformative message. Jesus lived his life alongside the poor and the marginalised, serving and loving with the Father's heart, and it is this same heart that is redeeming Rwanda: "Truly I tell you, whatever you did for one of the least of these brothers and sisters of mine, you did for me." (Matthew 25:40).

Often, though, it is the volunteers who find themselves profoundly touched and inspired by the healing and reconciliation that is happening in Rwanda, and the resilience of the Rwandan people. It is impossible not to be deeply humbled when, helping to lay bricks for a new kitchen, you find yourself standing between a woman whose husband was killed in the genocide and the wife of the man imprisoned for his murder. These volunteers are getting just a snapshot of the practical transformation that is happening, but all of this is only possible because of the work that has been done at the deepest heart level – uprooting, turning over and sifting through – sometimes over many years, to help people find personal healing, forgiveness, and the capacity to look forward with hope and expectation.

What characterises many of these initiatives, and sets them apart from what we might expect when we think of "community transformation" and "outreach projects", is that the focus is often just one individual or one family. A whole community (as well as international volunteers) comes together to build a stove, a kitchen, a toilet, or a home for just one genocide survivor, or one struggling family. Rabagirana and the local leaders don't assess "need" with a blanket view, spending years developing grandiose, large-scale projects with impressive, quantitative outputs that are going to change the shape of Rubavu overnight. Rather, it is about making one person's (or one family's) life easier, healthier and happier, and showing them that they are truly valued and loved; that they are not alone. That is world-changing for the individual, and when individuals are changed, communities are transformed.

Of course, there are also bigger, long-term projects and events to benefit the many. In recent years, MMI made an assessment with local government leaders that the mountain near Rubavu was eroding, and the proposed solution was to plant trees to slow the process down. However, this was a big job and required many hands. As well as members of the local community who were mobilised to help, along with local leaders and military personnel, the whole ISOR team came from Ndera, including many mzungu (even some French volunteers), as well as some Congolese. Given the historical relationship between Rwanda and France, and the potential for tension between Rwanda and Congo due to the refugee crisis, this was more than just an environmental necessity; the event created an opportunity to challenge stereotypes and change mindsets through working together. After the planting, Pastor Joseph of MMI addressed the group, highlighting the symbolism of this act of planting trees to safeguard for the future. The trees that now grow on that mountain are symbols of remembrance and peace: peace between individuals and peace between nations.

INCOME-GENERATING CO-OPERATIVES

Empowering people to be their own solutions to their problems has often taken the form of various co-operatives. After people have passed through the ministry of healing and reconciliation, they are brought together in groups according to their particular needs and skills. They decide what they want (and are able) to do, collectively, to generate income, and are trained by skilled volunteers.

One of the most successful co-operatives has been the Burinda group of widows and elderly women. The group was provided with three pigs initially, and when piglets were born they were distributed amongst the women. They each pay a small contribution to be part of the co-operative, and whenever a member's pig has piglets, she gives three away to other women in the group. One of the repercussions of such massive loss and displacement during the genocide is that it now falls to many of these older women to look after and provide for young children, and having a pig allows them to trade or sell for farming land, or for books, clothes or food for their grandchildren. They are truly an inspirational example to younger women – pulling together and working hard to support themselves and provide a better life for their families. Through a simple scheme, initiated with the logistical support and resources of the local government, they are empowered to be proactive and take responsibility for solving their own problems. In reality, the co-operative is not only a precious income-generating scheme, but it has grown into an invaluable support network, with the women meeting regularly, sharing struggles, and encouraging each other. As the pigs are quite literally handed from neighbour to neighbour, this builds a bridge, a connection, and even a close friendship, breaking the power of isolation and loneliness. This is a personal, organic process that bonds people in peace and unity.

The process of establishing, growing and supporting co-operatives has been a learning curve for all involved. Initially, MMI took responsibility for organising and instructing the groups, but this led to a dependency that was neither helpful nor sustainable. The initiatives needed to be owned by the community and they needed to feel empowered to take responsibility for themselves. Again, it was essential to engage the local government and church leaders to give people the opportunity, authority and resources to come up with their own ideas and set them in motion. Like any collaborative project, these co-operatives are not immune to internal disagreements or disorganisation, but if they are not proving successful, Rabagirana staff will work with local leaders and the church to support the group to pursue a new initiative and to work together more effectively. These local leaders regularly visit co-operatives to find out what they can do to support the growth and success of the project. Representatives from Rabagirana also take the opportunity to visit the co-operatives and to share the HWEC ministry with them for a day, for those who have yet to experience full personal healing, in order that these groups might be not just a practical inspiration but a shining light of God's love and redemption in their community.

POSITIONING LEADERS

Rabagirana seeks to inspire, educate and equip leaders in all areas of community life – health, education, local government and churches – to pioneer and support initiatives and developments, based on biblical principles. In this way, they are establishing a robust and sustainable framework for lasting change, and safeguarding the future of the nation.

Again, there is a strong focus on the responsibility of the Church to lead the way, and Rabagirana is working hard to empower the Church to become a transformative agent in communities. Pastors from different churches are brought together in discussion groups, to identify the problems and struggles in their own districts, and they then go out together to practically help families and rebuild communities. This expression of unity is almost as powerful, in itself, as their practical assistance, in rebuilding relationships, cultivating trust, and knitting communities back together.

Education is also pivotal for the future of Rwanda – for the nation to recover and to thrive. At the Rabagirana (formerly MMI) centre in Rubavu, the team is able to provide certain resources for students, teachers, pastors and local government leaders, equipping and investing in the influencers of today and the leaders of tomorrow. Computer facilities are available, as well as a small library, and there is also a literacy programme for volunteers, to train secondary school teachers. After visitors have received their training, or made use of the resources and facilities at the Rubavu centre, there is often the opportunity for them to experience some of the messages of HWEC; the leaders of the future need also to be healed and set free.

Rabagirana has recently celebrated its first graduation of empowered leaders from the newly established Bible College in Kigali. RBC offers academic programs in ministry, applied theology, leadership and organisation, and education, for students from all over Rwanda and the surrounding nations. Students can study for a one year certificate in Christian Ministry (in collaboration with Impact Christian University) or a three year Bachelor's degree in partnership with Logos University, USA. As well as an impressive academic qualification, students have the opportunity to improve their English and develop their IT skills, while gaining invaluable practical experience. The vision is that leaders would be trained and equipped with a Christian response to community challenges, a passion for holistic change, and the leadership skills to make a practical difference.

"LET US START REBUILDING." (NEHEMIAH 2:18)

When the imminent terror of the genocide subsided, it left in its wake a nation in complete shock: brokenness, woundedness, physical destruction, poverty, anxiety, fear and suspicion. Communities were utterly torn apart, and the prospect of starting to rebuild, restore and rise from the ashes seemed an insurmountable task. But just as Nehemiah surveyed the ruins of the wall of Jerusalem and set each man to work, side by side, taking responsibility for what lay in front of him (Nehemiah 3), so the work of rebuilding Rwanda began with individuals facing the brokenness on their own doorstep. And with each heart that is miraculously healed by the tender and transformational love of a faithful Father, a new pair of hands is added to the workers, and the vision of Rwanda as "a source of lasting peace, unity and light for the nations, to the glory of God" moves one step closer.

CHAPTER FOUR

We Are One

Our story began with God bringing an unlikely servant from North Wales, overwhelmed and out of her depth, to offer up what she had to give to the people of Rwanda and let Him do the rest. It wasn't long before the same was being asked of a musician and producer from We Are One Ministries, based in the small town of Malmesbury, UK. Dave Bankhead had been to South Africa with Rhiannon in 1998, and she had planted the seed of him coming to Rwanda with her at some point. Passionate about music and song-writing, and working out of a small studio in Malmesbury, Dave had long held a dream of using his skills, studio and equipment to help another developing culture in some way. It was a fairly vague, unformed dream, for sometime in the future perhaps, but when Joseph, Anastase and AEE sent him an invitation to come to Rwanda he suddenly faced the stark reality of seeing it through. The idea was to record and produce a CD of songs that expressed hope and healing for the nation.

MANA, KIZA U RWANDA (2000)

Initially, there was the inevitable question of funding the trip, but God was not going to allow money to be an obstacle. AEE had in fact been offered a huge sum from a Norwegian church association that had been given specifically for reconciliation through music, so the funds were available and Dave was willing. He was supported in prayer by his home church, Swindon Christian Fellowship, and was given one particular prophetic picture that would play a significant role in what was to come: a physical canopy of grace flowing out from the cross, covering all those who were sitting underneath it. Later, as he prepared to leave, the same friend from SCF showed up with a muslin sheet, saying, "You'll know when the right moment is, and what to do with it."

Arriving in Kigali, Dave and fellow musician Chip Bailey were taken to the church conference centre where they would be staying. Their fellow resident, a builder from South Africa, happened to mention that he had already had some trouble with his power tools blowing out and had had to buy a voltage regulator from a shop in town. This got Dave's attention as he started to worry about his own equipment, so he made sure to do the same. Even before the first session with the songwriters, God had his hand over Dave and his equipment, removing anything that might frustrate the good work he was there to do.

Joseph and Anastase had gathered together about 40 young worship leaders for this residential week, with the idea that they would have a handful of songs for a CD at the end of it. Dave had planned to spend the first three days dwelling on healing and reconciliation, and allow the songs to flow out of this place. He and Chip began by leading a time of worship – in the loosest possible sense! The group sang their own songs in their own language so it was more a case of catching what they were doing and supporting it from the keyboard and djembe. When he felt the time was right for something like the Cross Workshop, Dave remembered the picture he had been given of the canopy. During a break in the session, he, Joseph, Anastase and Rhiannon set up a large wooden cross with the vast muslin sheet flowing out from it as a covering.

When the group returned, Dave began to play and simply made space for people to personally and privately ask the Holy Spirit to reveal the pain and trauma in their own lives. He explained that they could symbolise this through the physical act of coming forward and sitting under the canopy, as a way of bringing it to the cross and releasing it to God. What followed was almost two hours of personal reflection, with people coming forward in ones, twos or small groups and being still under the covering of grace. There were tears, but it was quiet and a peace seemed to fill the room. For those two hours, nothing was said, but there was a real sense of people taking the time to privately consider their own thoughts, and their own hearts. It was only five years since the genocide, so people were still very nakedly traumatised and hadn't had an opportunity to come to terms with what had happened to them. It was so beyond anything of Dave's personal experience that he knew he had no words to offer. His role was not to comment, or to lead, but just to facilitate this time. Gradually, the atmosphere turned to one of celebration, and people started to sing.

The following day, Dave began the morning session by explaining the vision for the CD, but he found that the mood was very different to that of the previous day. There was some tension and suspicion in the air as some of the older pastors were sceptical of Dave's motives, concerned that he was an outsider who had seen an opportunity to make money out of their suffering. One pastor put this to him directly. Troubled by this response, Dave felt prompted to re-examine his own motives and be sure that he was involved for the right reasons. There were a lot of questions for him to answer and it wasn't an easy session, but he understood that white European men have given Rwandans many reasons to be suspicious and very few reasons to trust them. Still, it was a relief when one of the 16-year-old singers in the group raised her hand and asked, "When are we going to do the second CD?" Clearly, not everyone shared these reservations!

Eventually, Dave ran out of things to say and answers to give:

> I looked at the young people who had been with us up until that point and I said, "I don't want to defend what we're doing. I can't convince you. Why don't you ask the Holy Spirit if this is of God, and if He says yes, then come on the journey with us."

After a long lunch break, with much discussion and reflection, they came back together and agreed that this was what they wanted to do. The next step was to break down into songwriting groups. By this point, time was running short, but there was a fresh sense of enthusiasm and momentum in the room.

One of the singers to stand and share his song was Aimé Uwimana, who spoke humbly about how he had been holding onto a song called "Uwiteka Araje" ("The Lord is Coming") for two years because he felt that the Holy Spirit was telling him to wait until the time was right. During the course of this workshop he had realised that this was the moment he had been waiting for, and now was the time for this song to be heard. He started singing, and although it was in Kinyarwanda and Dave had no translation, the impact that it had on the others in the room was obvious. People were deeply moved and inspired by the words:

> Sing to the Lord a new song
> For He is coming to perform miracles in our country...
>
> Many nations will hear about our salvation
> They will proclaim that Rwanda has a wonderful God...

For a people that had long felt that the name of their nation had become a by-word for genocide, who hesitated to say that they were from Rwanda because it was such a terrible thing to put into words, the message of this song struck their hearts. Not knowing the words but understanding their meaning, etched on the faces of those around him, Dave knew they had found the first song for the CD.

Some other tracks came out of traditional Rwandan dance rhythms: the ikinimba (a vigorous, warrior-style of dance), the igyshakamba (brought to Rwanda from exiles in Uganda), and the umushayayo (celebrating unity). Anastase had the idea of setting words to these dances, and some of the group were absolutely in their element as they sang and praised, leading call and response. Although Dave loved this idea, it was a completely new challenge for him. He found himself trying to notate the rhythms for himself in shorthand, translating the beats, accents and cadences that seemed to live in the very bones of the Rwandan people into something that he could understand and recreate. He knew it was important to get this right; it had to be authentic and true.

Something special had been born that week, and as Dave said goodbye to Joseph and Anastase at the airport, none of them could have known how deep and how far it would take them. As they parted in tears, unable to find the words to express what they were feeling, all they knew was that God had faithfully knit them together and that they had started something good:

> It was just a miracle. There was a huge culture gap and I had never been there before, but it worked because God was determined to make it work. It was an amazing week.

Back in his studio in Malmesbury, Dave worked on the instrumental tracks for each of the songs, before returning to Rwanda to record the singers. As the reality of the finished album drew closer, Anastase felt that it wasn't enough to just distribute cassettes or CDs but that they should plan a proper launch event and really make a celebration of this amazing project. Ever the visionary, he booked the second largest stadium in the country for the event.

Having shipped three thousand physical copies of "Mana, Kiza U Rwanda" ("Lord, Heal Rwanda") over to Kigali, Dave prepared to return for a third time, with his wife, Jean, and colleagues Martin Neil (percussionist) and Steve Bassett (bassist and videographer). Friends at SCF made a huge banner for him to take with him, laying hands on it and praying over it, as a way of partnering with him and continuing to be a part of this amazing collaboration from across the many miles.

As well as a smaller event for VIPs at the Hôtel des Mille Collines, close to five thousand people attended the launch concert at Nyamirambo Stadium, and the singers performed with a freedom and a joy that was contagious. They just seemed so happy to be singing those words over their country, their leaders, their neighbours and their friends. The banner was paraded around the stadium, declaring, "Mana, Kiza U Rwanda!" in huge letters. Dave need not have worried about whether he had managed to recreate the authentic spirit of the dance tracks, as the singers and dancers seemed to know exactly what to do – and they just kept going! At the end of the day, as the equipment was packed up and the last of the crowds were leaving the stadium, still the young people kept singing, dancing and shouting their praise:

> It was something good in their lives and they were just going to celebrate it. We had spent eight hours performing, but far from being exhausted they were still singing at the tops of their voices as we drove away. There were lots of tears too. It was beyond words. God was doing something, and it was bigger than all of us.

On the way home, Dave and Jean had a stop-over in Nairobi so they took the opportunity to visit the national park. As they walked and reflected, Dave remembers the feeling of having been a part of something good, that had really made a difference. He was reminded of John 15:16: "I choose you and appointed you so that you might go and bear fruit – fruit that will last…"

> When God does something like that, it's just totally humbling. You know it's not you. I can't take any credit for it because there were so many things that were out of my control, that I couldn't have predicted.

Straight away, the album proved extremely popular in Rwanda, and was promoted on TV and radio. In 2001, they also toured the songs in concert, to Ruhengeri in the north and Butare in the south. Driving through the streets of Kigali, it was common to hear the familiar songs drifting out from one place or another, and they are played every year during the official mourning period in April. For worship leaders, in particular, it seemed to mark a transformational turning point, opening the way for them to write songs that truly express the reality of what life is like for them. It was also significant that the album was not attached to a particular choir, church, denomination or group. As Dave was an outsider, and the singers had been brought together as a one-off, there was no visible face behind it and it wasn't promoted with any particular agenda. It felt like the songs belonged to all Rwandans.

RABAGIRANA, RWANDA (2003)

Seeing the impact of this musical collaboration with Dave and We Are One, Joseph and Anastase were keen to follow up with a second album. Dave knew that they couldn't recreate the experience of making the first one, and it wasn't enough to just do the same thing again. It had to be something different. The first album had been so popular that he was also concerned about elevating the singers to superstar status and losing sight of the original vision. He suggested that the worship leaders who had been involved in the first album could write more songs for the second CD, but that this time they could be sung by children. So it was that, in 2002, Dave once again found himself leading a songwriting workshop.

Rhiannon had the idea of inviting a class from the local school to come in and talk to the songwriters, so a group of 12-year-olds joined them during the lunch break and the worship leaders were able to ask them questions, along the lines of: "When you think of your own future, what do you hope for?" Some of their answers were heartbreaking in their honesty. They hoped for things like "no more war" or "that I will never be thrown out onto the streets and become a street kid". The bar for their hopes and dreams was just so low, and some of the songwriters were painfully moved. It was clear to Dave that this had been the right thing to do, that it was really connecting, and that it was going to be very powerful in shaping the voice of this second album.

Sixty children, from eight years old and upwards, were brought together from local churches to sing the finished songs. This was a generation of children whose short lives had so far been dominated by genocide – either having lived through it, or having been born into its aftermath – and around 20 of them had been orphaned. Dave provided the rough backing tracks for them to rehearse with, while he worked on finishing and finalising these instrumental tracks back home. The process of getting the children ready for the recording was tough going, working with poor quality demos and equipment, so when Dave returned in August to record the singing he was met with quite a lot of concern from many of the mothers. He had a meeting with them and, touched by his contagious passion and excitement about the project, they seemed convinced that it could work.

This time, Dave had brought his oldest son with him to help with the recording and sound engineering. They worked with the children at the conference centre and in the recording studio, and the group sang with great confidence and conviction. All the time, Dave brought it back to the meaning of the words, and encouraged the children to talk about what they thought about the words they were singing. The launch for "Rabagirana, Rwanda" ("Arise, Shine, Rwanda") took place in January 2003, with two stadium concerts. These children are now in the their twenties and many are prominent worship leaders and songwriters. It was a deeply transformative experience for many of them, giving them a voice for their nation.

HAHIRW'ISHYANGA (2004)

By 2004, Antoine and AEE had seen the impact of the first two albums and were very keen to get involved, so many of the songs for "Hahirw'ishyanga" ("Blessed is the Nation") were written by staff members at AEE. They included titles such as "Umukiza W'Intimba" ("Healer of Grief"), "Dufite Intwari" ("We Have a Victor") and "Humura, Rwanda" ("Be Comforted, Rwanda"). Again, Dave faced a fresh musical challenge as Antoine wanted to incorporate the imvura rhythmic style, which has a very free tempo and is unlike anything that you would find in western music.

The tracks were recorded in February 2004, and the launch for this third album was incorporated into a wider mission by International AEE in 2005. Because of this, the numbers were huge, including many foreign delegates and church leaders from other African nations. Again, there was a concert for VIPs at the Hôtel des Mille Collines, but this time word spread that it would be attended by President Kagame himself. At the prayer breakfast, the choir performed some of the songs from the album, and the president was presented with a copy of all three healing and reconciliation CDs.

After Antoine had given a short speech, it was the turn of the president. He spoke clearly, in English, about his experience of leading the RPF into the country to put an end to the genocide in 1994. He remembered how they found whole villages that were completely deserted, in chaos, as people had fled. Looking inside people's huts they would often find Christian icons, crosses and Bibles strewn on the ground, and he said there was one question that had always stayed with him. In ten years, no-one had been able to give him an answer. Perhaps he was going off-script, or perhaps he had planned to say it, but he looked at the 150 pastors before him and asked: "Did those people also kill their neighbours?" That was what had haunted him and stayed with him, of all the terrible things he had seen. There was complete silence as the shame of the Church in Rwanda hung heavily in the room. Humanity failed during the genocide, and the Church failed with it. Thankfully, for all our sakes, that was not the end of the story.

At the stadium concert, with a crowd of eight thousand people, the marching band of the presidential guard paraded around the ground in full uniform, playing famous Christian hymns of peace and forgiveness, and the crowds cheered. The Amahoro Stadium had been the site of some of the most brutal events of the genocide, with the military playing a prominent role, and now these very people were honouring the Lord and celebrating his goodness in the stadium of peace. Watching from the sidelines, Dave felt an overwhelming sense that something was being born, but something was also coming to a close. This felt like the climax, and the end of a decisive chapter.

HEAL AFRICA (2005)

Dave has since re-recorded some of the most powerful tracks from the children's album, "Rabagirana, Rwanda", in English to give them wider scope and allow their powerful messages to speak to other peoples and nations. They were sung by an existing children's choir in South Africa, called Kidzing, but they also managed to raise the money to take six of the Rwandan children over to Johannesburg in order to keep that connection with the original album. "Heal Africa" was released in 2005, and some of the Kidzing children came over for a concert tour in 2008, performing in North Wales, Manchester, Swindon and Malmesbury. The final concert was packed with around four hundred people, many of whom had been supporting and praying for the ministry, through Dave, since the beginning.

Having dreamed, for many years, of using his gifts and resources to bless developing nations, it was almost as if this ministry took shape around Dave as he simply made himself available and held his own plans very loosely. He has gone on to hold similar songwriting workshops, alongside the HWEC ministry, in Burundi, Kenya, Côte d'Ivoire, Peru and Ukraine. The work is always shaped by the nation, the culture and the people involved, and no two missions are the same. There are always new rhythms to master, cultural differences to navigate and language barriers to overcome, but what Dave learned in Rwanda is that when God is in it, it bears fruit – fruit that will last.

CHAPTER FIVE

A Light to the Nations

So it is that God has knit this ministry together from so many drops in the ocean, so that it has started to spill over the borders of Rwanda into other areas where ethnic conflict and division have left their mark. Facilitators have been trained and teams have been commissioned in South Africa, DRC, Burundi, Kenya, Zimbabwe, Uganda, Sudan, and even beyond the borders of the African continent. Rabagirana estimates that at least one million people have been exposed to HWEC's message and work within Rwanda, and another one million internationally, through teams that have been trained up and sent out.

TO BURUNDI

Unlike in Rwanda, where Hutu politicians overthrew the Tutsi government in the elections after independence, in Burundi a joint Hutu and Tutsi party was formed. But tensions continued to rumble under the surface, periodically boiling over. The following decades were largely shaped by a severely unstable republic, with multiple coups and extreme ethnic violence, on both sides. The plane crash in April 1994 that killed both the Rwandan and Burundi presidents, and acted as a trigger to unleash the horrors of the Rwandan genocide, instead marked the beginning of a fifteen-year civil war in Burundi, with regional massacres of both Hutus and Tutsis. The peace agreement that was signed in May 2008 has again been threatened in recent years as President Pierre Nkurunziza ran for an unconstitutional third term in 2015, sparking protests, uprisings and outbreaks of violence once more. It is abundantly clear that, although Burundi avoided the devastation of genocide, the people have been no less wounded by relentless unrest and ongoing violence that gradually eats away at the fabric of communities, forcing people to "pick a side", corroding trust and diluting any hope for the future.

Teams were commissioned to take the HWEC ministry to Burundi in 2005, under the umbrella of AEE, and from 2008 it became part of Le Rucher Great Lakes Ministries. As in Rwanda, the initial focus was on the healing and reconciliation of individuals, and this was then followed up with community development and local initiatives. Partnering with Strategic Actions Network (SAN-Burundi), MMI first reached out to youth, students, young mothers and church leaders in Bujumbura and Gitega. Between July 2010 and July 2011, MMI supported AVD (Association des Volontaires pour le Development) and the Committee of Church Leaders for Reconciliation in Gitega, with financial support, resources and coaching, so that they would be in a position to run their own workshops, conferences and community projects and train up new facilitators.

Today, there are several local groups running HWEC workshops and promoting the real, living and breathing opportunity for healing and reconciliation, through churches and local NGOs. One of these is an organisation called "Cup of Cool Water", which was founded in Bujumbura in 2009 by Charles Ndikumana. Charles has been involved in the ministry of healing and reconciliation since 2005, in connection with AEE and World Outreach Initiative (WOI). When violence erupted in Burundi during the second democratic elections, and despair and hopelessness threatened to once again consume this troubled nation, Charles felt that God was calling him to show people that there was a way to heal the wounds of this long-standing ethnic conflict.

Between 2005 and 2009, approximately twelve thousand people received the message of healing and reconciliation, including many church leaders, governors, local authorities, members of the Ministry of Good Governance, members of former armed groups and the army itself, teachers, leaders of Christian organisations, widows, orphans and youth. Charles and his team were trained by both AEE and MMI and he is still working closely with Rabagirana as the co-ordinator of the Burundian HWEC Forum.

Francine took part in the Training of Facilitators in Burundi in June 2010, and she tells of how God utterly transformed her heart and her mind through the Cross Workshop:

> Before my inner wounds were healed, I saw the Hutu as animals because of all I had learned about them in my family. I will never forget how my father died, killed by Hutu rebels, and I and my siblings became orphans. Later on, our house and other possessions were destroyed by them. When my sister decided to marry a Hutu, I became very angry and decided to disappear, thinking that I would come back for vengeance. But finally, in this workshop, God touched my heart. I knew that the Hutu were created by God, just as the Tutsi were, and that they are as good as the Tutsi. I could see many, many good things in the Hutu. At the end of the seminar my heart was fine; I forgave the Hutu and received a new love from God for them.

TO THE DEMOCRATIC REPUBLIC OF CONGO

The DRC is a vast and sprawling nation, with hundreds of different ethnic groups, languages, religions and classes. As is sadly typical of the colonial era in Africa, this diversity was exploited and manipulated so that ethnic differences and inequalities were reinforced and entrenched by the time that independence was achieved in 1960. Amidst the struggle for power and control that inevitably followed, the nation suffered from broiling ethnic tensions and brutal civil war. In 1994, this was intensified by the influx of hundreds of thousands of Hutu refugees and extremists, pouring over the borders from Rwanda and Burundi as the situations became toxic in their home nations. In fact, the interventions and influences of surrounding regions (Angola, Namibia, Rwanda, Uganda and Zimbabwe among them) have played a large part in creating a lingering atmosphere of insecurity and unrest. The International Rescue Committee reported that, between 1998 and 2004, almost four million people died as a result of civil war in DRC.

It is telling that the various armed rebel groups that have emerged and clashed in DRC define themselves along predominantly ethnic lines. In 2007, there was a particular resurgence of violence between Congolese Tutsi and Rwandan Hutu Interahamwe in Kivu, eastern DRC; another after-shock of the events in Rwanda in 1994 as the Congolese Tutsi minority had long felt that their security was under threat, and the Rwandan genocide only confirmed their worst fears.

Having heard some of the stories of healing and reconciliation coming out of a reeling Rwanda in the aftermath of the genocide, the leader of the Christian organisation Groupe d'Action Socio-Agro Patoral (GASAP), Theofile Gakunzi, invited the team to run a HWEC workshop in South Kivu in 1999. Around 40 pastors and local leaders took part, and more workshops soon followed. In Bukavu, the ministry culminated in an opportunity for participants to share their testimonies in various churches, so that around a thousand people of different tribes were exposed to the HWEC teaching and the stories of how God was using it to bring transformation. Since then, many Christian leaders in the region have been trained as facilitators. GASAP has adopted the HWEC material, holding seminars and rallies for reconciliation, and helping farmers from different tribal communities to work together.

In 2001, the finance manager at the mission hospital of Nyankunde (Centre Médical Évangelique) in North Kivu, Daniel M. Kaseraka, was presented with three HWEC booklets. Daniel is an ardent evangelist and had led a significant ministry of intercession in the region. The booklets were brought to his attention by Medair (the same Christian relief organisation responsible for inviting Rhiannon to Rwanda in 1994). He was astounded by the teaching and felt that it was exactly what they had been waiting and praying for in the region. Invigorated, he invited Rhiannon to run a HWEC workshop and it was planned for November 2002, but – in a cruel twist of irony – it was the very urgency of the need for this ministry that reared its head in a catastrophic way and ended up delaying it. In September, the conflict and violence in the area escalated, the hospital was razed to the ground and over a thousand people were killed in Nyankunde.

Finally, in August 2004, Rhiannon was able to come to DRC to hold a HWEC workshop for key Christian leaders from different churches. Afterwards, there was a real sense of hope and anticipation for all that might be possible: "With this teaching we can stop the war!" More than six hundred local intercessors were trained as facilitators and the teaching spread through the villages and communities of north and east DRC. In October, Daniel himself travelled to Le Rucher in Geneva, where he spent a month being trained in the HWEC material and equipped with the principles and processes of community development. The progress in DRC has been especially powerful and encouraging. In March 2007, 72 regional chiefs and leaders from various villages went through the HWEC workshop and were utterly transformed. With civil war still raging around them, these chiefs repented, forgave and were reconciled, and a week later the fighting in the region came to an end.

Some of the leaders of the demobilising militia groups, tired and disillusioned with the fight, reached out to the facilitators and actually requested specific workshops for militia on both sides of the conflict. Predictably, the first workshop got off to a rocky start, with accusations, abuse and demands flying in all directions. This soon settled into an uneasy calm, and by the time it came to the Cross Workshop, everyone in the room was brought to their knees. Approaching the King's table in the Holy Nation, at the end of the workshop, the participants rushed to assemble a further two thousand militia who were in need of this ministry. Between January 2009 and December 2011, 20 HWEC workshops were held for members of disarmed militia units and hundreds have since become ambassadors for peace, travelling to the very villages that they ravaged, confessing publicly and asking for forgiveness. These workshops were organised by Organisation Évangélisation Intercession Libération (OEIL), with the support of MMI.

Originally focusing on church leaders and Christian communities, OEIL then extended the ministry to local authorities and ex-combatants. As in Rwanda, they recognised the broader, lingering consequences of such ongoing violence, instability and poverty in the lives of families and communities, and began to reach out to the youth in particular. In partnership with the Université Chretienne Bilingue du Congo (UCBC), a member of OEIL staff acts as a chaplain for the students, and they are able to teach the HWEC material to every student as part of the curriculum. Many young people, born into conflict or simply growing up in wounded communities and traumatised nations, will not even be consciously aware of the scars they inherit, but allowing them to lie dormant and fester is only to delay the inevitable consequences. OEIL has organised many HWEC workshops for high school graduates and is working on integrating this material into primary schools and adapting workshops for Sunday schools, in order to reach children of all ages in the most natural and appropriate way. They are also training many secondary school teachers as facilitators so that they can incorporate these teachings, messages and activities into their daily lessons.

The situation in DRC today is sadly still fraught and volatile, with government corruption, poverty, a lack of education and opportunity, and new militia groups continuing to form. Recently, more mass graves have been uncovered. There is clearly still a lot of work to be done but, as Daniel Kaseraka puts it:

> It is a soul winning business. If it was a secular organisation, I could not do all this work, but I know that in the end what we are doing is building God's Kingdom. Evangelism is my life; wherever I go, Jesus has to be known first.

TO UGANDA

The region that the British colonisers, somewhat arbitrarily, delineated as what we now call Uganda bundles together a wide range of ethnic groups, political systems, cultures and religions – and the story is all too familiar. Favouring the Baganda as their primary allies, the colonial rulers cultivated an environment of resentment and division, and attempted to restructure the country around an export of the Westminster model of parliamentary democracy. The first Ugandan politicians to take office in 1962, after independence, were therefore faced with an entirely alien political system for which they were ill-equipped and inexperienced. The Prime Minister, Milton Obote, faced violent protests, riots and military coups as he attempted to consolidate his power. Obote's army commander, General Idi Amin Dada, overthrew the Prime Minister in 1971 and what followed was essentially a reign of terror.

Amin tortured or killed his opponents, anyone who appeared to stand in his way, and especially those who had shown support for Obote. The entire population of ethnic Asians living in Uganda was violently evicted, and hundreds of thousands are thought to have been killed under Amin's rule. Defeated by a Tanzanian invasion in 1978-9 Amin fled to Libya, and in a corrupt electoral process Obote returned to office in 1980. Again, the Ugandan people suffered under a brutal rule, characterised by abuse, rape, torture, corruption and destruction. In 1986, Yoweri Museveni, who had resisted and fought the regimes of both Obote and Amin, came to power and the situation began to improve.

Decades of brutality, repression and human rights abuses have left their mark, though, and unrest has continued between government forces and rebel armies in the northern territories. The first HWEC team came to Uganda in 2008 to hold a workshop for church leaders from various denominations in Gulu, and it became apparent to the facilitators from MMI that some of the most fraught tensions existed along a north/south divide in the country. Many of the northerners felt oppressed, and there was a lot of resentment against the government. The problem, at this first workshop, was that there was no-one to stand in the gap and speak on behalf of the southerners, so the team expanded the ministry into the south of the country. The workshop in Masaka in 2010, however, revealed that many of those in central and southern Uganda were more concerned about tensions and prejudices between the various ethnic groups living alongside each other in these areas – particularly between the Baganda and Banyarwanda (Rwandans living in exile). So it wasn't until October 2011 that representatives from Gulu and Masaka were brought together for a Training of Facilitators, and found that they could be united in their vision and hope for their country.

Local groups continue to promote the ministry in both Gulu and Masaka, and to incorporate the teaching into sermons, Bible studies, and within their own families and relationships. Alice, a teacher in Gulu, shares how the ministry has been transformative for some of the children at her school:

> Many come from broken homes and are bitter so reconciliation is needed, first, in the families. So I take the teachings down to the level of the children. We sit together on the floor and I share what the Bible says about conflict and the goodness of having joy. I teach about reconciliation: that the friend who you hurt is also the friend who could help you, so we need to live reconciled, and so on.
>
> Once I had a child who was having troubles at home: the father used to beat them up and chase them away. So I called and involved the parents. I taught about conflict and God's intentions, and we talked and prayed together. The parents finally reconciled and had joy again; they started laughing together! Still, today, they are living together in harmony. The father has stopped beating and chasing away his child.

Emboldened by the impact they have seen so far, the team in Gulu is excited to reach out to other northern districts, and even to South Sudan, although financial resources are still limited. The Masaka group has found that tribal divisions, prejudices and suspicions are strong and persistent, even within churches and between pastors. The HWEC workshops have been a powerful tool but the team is stretched to capacity because there are so many who are desperate for this message of reconciliation. They are keen to become more organised, structured and effective in spreading this ministry, and to train up more church leaders as facilitators. They have not struggled, though, to mobilise people once they have experienced the power of the ministry for themselves.

TO KENYA

One of the primary legacies of colonial rule in Kenya was the British acquisition of the fertile land of the Rift Valley for themselves, stripping many Kikuyu landowners of their property and expelling pastoral communities like the Kalenjin and Maasai. They also forcefully enlisted thousands of Kikuyu, Luhya, Luo and Kisii to come and work for them in the Rift Valley, thus blindly and irreversibly confusing the socio-cultural make-up of Kenya and abusing this fruitful land to their own ends.

After a bloody uprising and civil war, in protest against colonial rule and the controversial land policies, the independent Republic of Kenya was established in 1964. The Kikuyu president, Jomo Kenyatta, was careful to include representatives of other ethnic groups in his administration, and to consider the interests of the African, Asian and European communities living in Kenya. After his death, however, he was succeeded by Daniel Arap Moi, a Kalenjin from the Rift Valley. Concerned about holding on to his power, Moi was intolerant of any form of opposition. In 2002, Mwai Kibaki was elected, bringing Moi's rule to an end.

The 1990s saw ethnic tensions flare between Kalenjin and Kikuyu, and the elections in particular often prompted violent outbreaks. Between 1992 and 1993, during the first multi-party elections, approximately 1,500 people were killed as a result of ethnic conflict, with the Rift Valley being the eye of the storm. In 2001 and 2005, again, thousands were killed, left homeless or displaced because of ethnic clashes. The elections of 2007 were particularly controversial, prompting two months of violent atrocities, chaos and unrest, until a power-sharing agreement was signed. The new coalition government then had to deal with the challenges of resettling those who had been displaced, and bringing judicial proceedings against those responsible for the violence. The Truth, Justice and Reconciliation Commission was one attempt by the government at helping the country to process its history and begin to heal, and the National Cohesion and Integration Commission promoted national unity and peace, but it has not been a smooth journey and the fear of a resurgence of violence lingers on.

The first HWEC workshop was held in Nakuru in 2008, supported by Tearfund UK. Rhiannon came from Wales, Joseph Nyamutera from Rwanda, and Daniel Kaseraka from Congo, to facilitate. The Anglican Church of Kenya and the Mother's Union had gathered some of the most wounded and traumatised people from various communities, and many were unsure about what kind of workshop they were attending. Initially shocked that they were being asked to sit in the same room as members of these other ethnic groups, they soon engaged with the teaching and, by the end, were even able to call their fellow participants friends.

Three months later, fifteen of these first participants were invited back to be trained as facilitators, so that they could take the workshops to their own communities and home churches. These facilitators have since been invited to speak at various events and ACK Mother's Union conferences, and to run the workshops in churches across the country, in partnership with the Anglican Church and supported by Tearfund UK. Between 2008 and 2011, it is estimated that more than eight hundred church and community leaders have been reached with the message of healing and reconciliation. In 2011, with the support of Rhiannon and Joseph, they formed their own NGO, called "Way of Peace (WAPE)". Through small healing workshops and local initiatives, they have reached more than 55,000 people and have some incredible testimonies to show for it, including members of criminal gangs openly repenting.

In November 2011, the team organised a huge event in the town of Eldoret – one of the areas that had been most damaged and traumatised by the violence around the elections. The 11/11 Mother's Union Peace Prayer Rally included sixteen HWEC workshops with around four hundred participants, as well as sports tournaments that brought together young people from many different communities. Some two thousand people filled the stadium for the main rally, and Rhiannon stood in the gap on behalf of the British colonial powers, washing the feet of some of her Kenyan colleagues in a powerfully symbolic and emotive act. An elderly Kikuyu man, after having his feet washed, describes the effect it had on him:

> Even at this age I am so blessed to see this change in me! I have been to many workshops but none like this. I can even jump for joy now! This has turned my world upside down. We were all divided, even as Kikuyu. I fought during the Mau Mau uprising. Even in 2007, I had influenced young people to fight. My nickname is "hard rock" but my heart came back to me yesterday. Now I'm at peace with everybody. My heart is cleansed. Everyone is my brother. I'm now going back to influence the young people by modelling peace.

Dr. Allan Waihumbu, Director of WAPE, beautifully expresses their ongoing mission:

> What Kenya went through is not a scenario anyone would ever wish to happen again. Therefore, every moment, every opportunity, every resource available we want to see invested. If only one person per workshop is healed and becomes an agent for transforming others in that area, it is worth everything. As soon as one area is healed, healing will spread to other areas so that, at some point, we will have a majority of healed areas in our country and the problem of post-election violence or ethnic conflict will be over.

As a follow-up to the HWEC workshops, WAPE also works in partnership with the Kenyan government to offer a training programme in Good Governance and Civic Education. The curriculum – covering leadership, accountability and electoral process – is provided by the government but is grounded in biblical principles.

These workshops have been offered to influential local leaders in particular hotspot areas to encourage informed involvement in political processes, and peaceful elections.

TO SOUTH AFRICA

The divisive history of South Africa is well-documented. Apartheid entered official policy in 1948, with the African National Congress (ANC), and prominent figures such as Nelson Mandela, leading the opposition. The first multi-racial elections took place in 1994 and saw an ANC-led government bring an end to apartheid. Of course, these things are never so simple to undo, and the legacy of prejudice and division lingered on in the form of inequalities in housing, education, healthcare and life opportunities. Broadly speaking, while the majority black African population gained political power, the white Afrikaners still have an economic advantage, while coloured Africans, and Indian and Asian peoples straddle the awkward middle-ground.

As the long and laborious process of restitution drags on – returning land that was seized during apartheid back to its previous owners – many black South Africans feel angry and disillusioned at the slow pace of change, while Afrikaners feel increasingly vulnerable as a minority in the country. Many young white people, for their part, are frustrated at having to pay the price for apartheid, particularly in the form of the inequality of higher level education and career opportunities available to them, as a result of Black Economic Empowerment. The wounds of apartheid run deep, and are constantly poked and prodded by the growing rich/poor divide, widespread corruption and high crime rates.

The Truth and Reconciliation Commission, led by Archbishop Desmond Tutu, was hugely valuable in giving victims a platform to tell their stories of discrimination and suffering, and for perpetrators to repent, but it was more of a restorative justice process than an opportunity for individual healing. Antoine put it this way: "I believe South Africa is peacefully co-habiting rather than being peacefully reconciled."

The HWEC ministry was invited to South Africa in 1997, and Mercy Ministries South Africa (MMSA) was established in 2001. The team realised quite quickly that the word "reconciliation" was off-putting for many people as they assumed there was a political motive, so alternative vocabulary was needed when promoting the ministry. Workshops were initially run for church leaders, who were then trained as facilitators to present the material to their congregations. It proved difficult, at first, to get ministers on board, so the team started by offering the loss and bereavement element of the HWEC material as a one-day workshop. They found that people could identify with this and were more ready to recognise their need for this teaching, so it offered a way in to the HWEC ministry as a whole.

As a result of the workshops, several inter-ethnic prayer groups have formed to intercede for their communities. People of different ethnic groups are partnering around a shared heart for healing and reconciliation in their communities. Maria dos Santos, who joined the team in 2005, has also adapted the format of the workshops for youth camps, adding some extra topic areas and even incorporating relevant movies to prompt discussion around themes of reconciliation.

One particular church in Kempton Park was so impacted by the workshop that they felt called by God to welcome people of all ethnic groups at their services, and they now run one service in English and one in Afrikaans. In another powerful example of God's endless capacity for healing and restoration, a farming community in De Doorns, in the Western Cape, took part in a workshop together – farmers alongside their labourers – which culminated in them washing each other's feet. There are countless examples of people standing up and sharing about the hatred they used to feel for those of another ethnic group, until God healed their hearts and opened their eyes to the individuals standing before them. At the end of one particular workshop in the Rocky Valley, a young man who fought passionately against apartheid looked one of the white men in the face and said:

> Before, you were my enemy but today you have become my brother, and if anyone wants to hurt you they will have to come through me. Today we are writing a new history, and it is not written in books but on the rocks and stones here at Rocky Valley.

TO ZIMBABWE

The largest ethnic groups in Zimbabwe are the Shona (around 82%) and Ndebele (related to the Zulu of South Africa). Robert Mugabe's ZANU-PF party (Zimbabwe African National Union – Patriotic Front) has held the vast majority of the power since the mid-1980s. Its main opposition has been the Movement for Democratic Change (MDC), which finds particularly strong support in the Ndebele heartlands of Zimbabwe. ZANU-PF's consolidation of power, itself, has left lasting wounds as it was bloodied by a brutal genocide of Ndebele communities by Mugabe's 5th Brigade in 1985, known as the Gukurahundi.

As the people of Zimbabwe go about their day to day lives, there has long been an undercurrent of discontent, frustration and disappointment that independence has not brought with it the freedom and opportunity for all that it promised. Instead, they have faced government corruption, inflation, unemployment, and insecurity. Elections in Zimbabwe have been plagued with outbreaks of violence and intimidation, and reports of fixed polling results. Particularly extreme violence erupted around the 2008 elections, reportedly resulting in up to one hundred deaths and many more wounded and displaced, and prompting condemnation from the international community.

White Zimbabweans make up only about 1% of the population, but historically they have owned much of the land and profitable farms. After ZANU-PF's land resettlement programme collapsed under the weight of corruption, mismanagement and government inertia, frustrations and resentments grew, eventually bubbling over into an illegal invasion of many farms in 2000. White farmers were forced from their land with no compensation, and some were even chased from the country. Ethnic tensions in Zimbabwe are therefore ripe and complex, and all the more so because they are so thoroughly intertwined with political conflict.

Rhiannon led the first HWEC workshop in Zimbabwe in 2009, with the support of Tearfund. Thirty-five participants – a mixture of Shona and Ndebele – took part. The breakthrough came as Rhiannon stood in the gap and repented to the people of Zimbabwe for the actions and abuses of white British colonialists, asking for their forgiveness. This was a powerful moment of confession, and as the Shona and Ndebele participants stood side by side to offer their forgiveness to the British, they also found that they were able to confront the divisions between themselves. By the end of the workshop they were washing one another's feet.

In September of that year, Joseph and Rhiannon ran a Training of Facilitators for fourteen Christian leaders in Bulawayo. The participants ended up forming three teams and, funded by Tearfund, some began to run workshops that specifically focused on the political conflict in the country, in anticipation of the elections of 2012. They approached some prominent political leaders and brought together supporters of opposing parties, shifting the emphasis away from ethnic differences and onto conflict in general. They found that they needed to initially leave aside the sessions on the Holy Nation and Standing in the Gap in order to focus on the more immediate political differences, and instead ran a series of ten workshops on "Healing the Wounds of Political Conflict". The Cross Workshop was especially well received and had a profound impact on people. There is still a need to return to the original vision of the HWEC ministry, but the opportunities for speaking openly about ethnic divisions are heavily dependent on the political situation. Following the dramatic political changes that have come about for Zimbabwe in 2017, with the momentous resignation of Mugabe, perhaps some doors will start to open in the near future. Only time will tell.

BEYOND THE BORDERS

But this outpouring of hope, redemption, healing and reconciliation is bigger than the continent of Africa, and cannot be contained by borders. Already, the ministry is making waves as far afield as Hungary, Ukraine, Afghanistan and Sri Lanka, starting with individuals but transforming nations.

One of the key ways in which Rabagirana has been able to reach others around the world who could benefit from the transformational HWEC ministry is through the International School of Reconciliation (ISOR), which was established in partnership with Le Rucher Ministries. This is an annual programme that runs for 22 days and takes participants through three stages: the HWEC workshop, practical community development projects, and leader development training. International leaders and representatives are invited to take part through Rabagirana's far-reaching network of partnerships and connections with other reconciliation organisations and interested parties. So far, eighteen countries have been represented at ISOR, including delegates from as far afield as Afghanistan, Nepal and Myanmar.

The school brings together an eclectic blend of global participants to engage in personal healing ministry, structured teaching, visits to memorials, outreach work with victims and perpetrators, and practical community development. Every other year, representatives from nations and communities that have been ripped apart by conflict are drawn to the heart of Rwanda to stand side by side and experience the power of connection, unity, peace and hope for the future. In the interim years, the school re-locates to be hosted by another nation, at the request of a representative who has passed through the programme. There are also several forums and conferences throughout the year to extend these global connections, build bridges between nations, and promote the message that we are united in our pursuit of peace and reconciliation.

When participants take the experience of ISOR back to their home nations and start to live it out, it has proven to have powerful repercussions, even beyond the issue of ethnicity. Omer expresses it eloquently when he says, "You can see the wholeness in it." He explains that some participants have found that the teaching about reconciliation has helped them to live well with their husband or wife, or to manage their employees fairly and effectively. The HWEC material seems to minister to all aspects of people's lives, helping them to live peacefully with those around them.

A BEACON OF HOPE

At the centre in Masaka, Rabagirana has also established an immersive exhibition called the Reconciliation Lighthouse, which guides visitors on a visual and reflective journey through the process of healing and reconciliation. There is a path to follow, with various "stations", each marked by a striking work of art. The artists have all taken part in a HWEC workshop and have then been invited to express their reflections through their artistic creations. This gives visitors a touchpoint for acknowledging and processing their own experiences of woundedness, healing and reconciliation. Omer describes the physical journey through the stations as a reflection of the journey of HWEC:

> It is a path interrupted by stations, and each station has its own message. It is a kind of summary of the "Healing the Wounds of Ethnic Conflict" message. For example, the first station is celebrating diversity, and it is a summary of one of the topics we have in the book of HWEC. There is also a bit about prejudice, and a wounded heart... After that, there is a healing station, where we talk about the power of the cross: that the cross is there to help us to be healed. Then comes the part of reconciliation where we see forgiveness,

> repentance, and standing in the gap, where you can confess on behalf of your group. Then we go to the other station, which is the Holy Nation, where we celebrate our diversity: we value everyone and we affirm one another.

Conceived out of Rabagirana's vision that Rwanda would be "a light to the nations", the hope is that the Reconciliation Lighthouse would be a beacon for other weary travellers as they navigate the murky and perilous waters of post-conflict trauma, showing them the way, and guiding them safely home.

CHAPTER SIX

Looking Forward, Looking Up

When I asked Elia what he thinks the world needs to learn from Rwanda, this is what he told me:

> The reconciliation that happened in this country is not supposed to be a mystery to outsiders. It is something tangible; it's a real life story that actually happened… So if the whole world is looking at Rwanda, they should learn a big lesson. I should now be living in fear. I should be afraid to go into the forest for fear of meeting a relative of the guy I killed, but now I don't have that fear, and what made that possible was the reconciliation that happened between the Rwandan people.

It is not supposed to be a "mystery". We are not supposed to just shake our heads and say, "Well, that's an incredible story. I could never do that, but good for them." For those of us on the outside, perhaps we would prefer to think that what happened during the genocide was down to some weakness in the Rwandan spirit, rather than a flaw in human nature itself. Perhaps it was something specific to those people, in that place, at that time, and we need only look on with compassion. But the facts just don't fall that way. While most of us cannot know for sure how we would respond in a similar situation, and of course there were specific factors that contributed to this particular disaster, we cannot ignore the overwhelming evidence that the same frailties and weaknesses of the human condition, the same human fears and vulnerabilities that were exposed during the Rwandan genocide, exist in all of us.

We want to belong, to know where we stand, and all too often this seems to come at the cost of shutting others out. Keeping a grip on our own security, power or material comfort becomes more important than compassion, equality, friendship, and love. Being accepted by the group takes precedence over speaking up for the one. Diversity is held up as something to be discouraged, even feared. We're afraid of people who are different to us, and we're afraid that if others have more, we'll have less. If we feel insecure enough, scared enough, angry enough, who's to say what our limits are? And one of the lessons that Rwanda has to teach us is that when neighbour turns against neighbour, everyone loses. No-one comes out of it unscathed. The wounds run deep and it is a long road back.

But if Rwanda's past exposes our greatest weaknesses, her present and her future are shining a light on our greatest source of strength: these people were not born with a gene for genocide, but neither do they have an innate capacity for forgiveness or a superhuman ability to rise from the ashes that is uniquely Rwandan. The impressive rebuilding of the nation itself, and the outpouring of reconciliation that is transforming lives, is testament to something that is available to all of us. This same power, in all its glory, is ours. This is the truth that Rwanda bears witness to: that there is a way to rebuild what was broken and to restore what was lost. When neighbour stands with neighbour, who's to say what our limits might be?

When Jesus said, "But I tell you, love your enemies and pray for those who persecute you" (Matthew 5:44), he knew what he was asking of us. He, of all people, knew what it meant to be persecuted and driven to a brutal death at the hands of his neighbours, because of their fear, confusion and mistrust. As he drew his final breaths, he prayed for them because, even at their most inhumane, he still saw them as human, afraid of something they didn't understand, and – after all – he loved them. This is our example of forgiveness that is not deserved, of love that is not earned, of life that conquers death. This is what makes it possible for a mother to look a man in the eye, a man who handed her children over to death, and see someone who is deeply broken. This is how a Tutsi woman can look at her Hutu husband and see nothing but the man she loves, the father of her children. This is how a woman who saw her children massacred, and endured being burned alive in her house, can say, "I am so happy. God has redeemed that pain into something good." Once a shell, with open wounds, whose very name was cloaked in shame, Rwanda is now a nation with a hope and a future.

Having attended the HWEC workshop in Nakuru, Kenya, James Gichogo Chacha spoke words so profound that there is nothing more to say:

> God has given me more than I lost.

What a promise. What a hope.

Acknowledgements

I will always be thankful to Joseph Nyamutera for inviting me to play a small part in this great story, as well as all those who hosted us, prepared food for us, drove us around, and generously gave their time in practical ways to welcome us to Rwanda. I would also like to mention Esther Hamm, whose thorough and conscientious research proved invaluable to this project.

A particular appreciation must go to our outstanding translators, who sat with us for many hours in total, having to bear the burden of communicating sometimes unspeakable testimonies to make this work possible. They were patient and diligent, and I am deeply grateful.

A huge thank-you to Simon Baker, Matt Withers, and all those who proofread, gave feedback, and contributed to turning this incredible story into something that you can hold in your hand.

Above all, I would like to thank the kind, humble and courageous people who shared their intensely personal stories with us in the hope that they might inspire and encourage others. They were hard to hear but, I'm sure, far harder to tell.

APPENDIX

Testimonies

The following are transcriptions of interviews carried out in and around Kigali in February 2015. Sometimes we spoke in English and on other occasions we had the help of a local translator.

OMER

Have you always lived in Rwanda?

I was born as a refugee. My father was a Burundian and he fled here, to Rwanda, in 1972 because of ethnic conflict between the Tutsi and the Hutu in Burundi. When he arrived in Rwanda he married a Rwandan woman, and I was born as a refugee. As I was growing up, we started to ask our father many questions: "Why are we called Burundian?" "Why are we in Rwanda?" What was happening? My dad told us that it was because of ethnic conflict between the Hutu and the Tutsi in Burundi, and that as he was a Hutu, he was chased away; he was forced to flee to Rwanda. I started to think that Tutsis were, perhaps, bad people, and that they didn't want Hutus to be alive, or to prosper in their lives. So, in my heart, at a young age, I started to feel hatred towards Tutsis. This came out when I was at primary school: we would beat Tutsi classmates, we were angry with them, we turned against them. We could not see any good in them because of that hatred.

But things grew worse when a Hutu president was elected in 1993, and as we were refugees, we hoped that we might go back to our country after the election. Many Rwandans came to my dad in that time and offered to buy the property from him, because a Hutu president had been elected and they thought that we were ready to go back home to Burundi. As children, we were very excited to go and see our cousins, and our uncles. But my dad told them: "I know Tutsis are tricky. They will kill that president. Wait for three or four months and then we'll see what is going on. If the president is still alive, maybe something positive will happen."

Unfortunately, three months later, he was killed. For me, it was a sort of confirmation of what I had felt towards Tutsis. In that time, we were very angry. My dad was very angry. But even though he told us that the Tutsis were against him, he didn't particularly encourage us to treat them badly; he just gave us the information and we interpreted it how we wanted.

Then the RPF attacked Rwanda and there was a war. The rumours were that Tutsis wanted to invade Rwanda, and all of that confirmed and amplified how I felt. I was very angry, but I was only 11 or 12 years old. In 1994, after the genocide, we fled to Congo. One week later, my dad died. At that time, we were very angry. It was the second country in which we were refugees. For me, it was really bad. Even though I was very young, I could feel the weight of being a refugee in a second country.

Some Burundians called us together, and they said: "You see, we are nothing now. We are worse than defeated. It is like we don't have the right to be in this world. So let's try to fight so that we can go to Burundi. At least let's die in Burundi, not in Congo, in exile, because this is the second country, and this is really too much. And the people who are causing us this misery are the Tutsis. So let's try to contact Hutu militias of Rwanda. They will train us in the military, and after being trained, we will help them to go back into Rwanda, and after that we'll go straight to Burundi and fight there. At least let's die there." In Burundi, already, there were militias who were trying to fight against the government, and they said we should go and join them.

At 13 years old I joined the training. For three months, I think, I was the little one among the others. They were 20 and 25 years old, and I was 13. Then, about one week before we were going to infiltrate Rwanda, Congo was attacked, and when war broke out in Congo, that put an end to our ambitions, and I was very angry. I didn't have any political intention. For me, it was hatred. I was driven by hatred alone: fighting and killing. I said to myself: "My enemy is the Tutsi." I didn't think about political leaders; no, just the Tutsi. I was very angry that we had been prevented from carrying out our plans. When war broke out there, we could not organise ourselves to go to the front because we had to care for our families, we had to care for our little brothers. So because of that, I was prevented.

After four to six months, I was back in Rwanda with my mum: because she was Rwandan, I had the right to be a Rwandan, as is stated in the constitution. When I was in Rwanda, the first thing I had in my mind was: "I am not permitted to be in Rwanda, because I am a Hutu, and the country is for Tutsi." And there was a genocide: we were guilty, and we carried the shame of what had been done on our part, as Hutus. We were just guilty, with no hope. We were reduced to nothing.

Then, after I got saved, I received Jesus as my Lord, and from that point I started to see a difference. I started to see Tutsis coming to minister to me, helping me, giving me clothes. As we were coming from Congo, from exile, we didn't have anything but our dirty clothes, so they tried to help us. We were thrown together in the church, and I started to have a kind of renewal of the mind. But it didn't really help me much, to heal me or to help me to deal with my background, because my dad died without bringing us to Burundi. So it was still burning in my heart.

Another problem was that our names express the suffering of my dad. My big sister is called, in Kinyarwanda, Ytonde, which means:

"Be careful, be careful. This is not your country." So it reminds you every day that this is not your country, and it reflects my dad's suffering. I am called Mayobera, which means: "mysterious". I was born when my dad was coming back from Burundi and, as my mother told me, when he returned he said there was no hope that we could go to Burundi, because there was still hatred and ethnic division. So he was confused, and he called me "mysterious, mystery". My little brother's name is Dogidogi. Dogidogi is a Kinyarwanda name, or Kirundi name, but it means: "Slowly, slowly, slowly". This name is very, very bad, because my dad gave him that name when some Hutus tried to attack Burundi in 1989/86/87, and they killed many Tutsis in the north of Burundi, and my dad felt like: "Maybe, slowly, slowly, bit by bit, maybe we can do something to claim our right." And our youngest: she's called Kebeya. Kebeya means: "I don't know where I am coming from, and I don't know where I am going." Totally confused; without hope.

So those names reflect the suffering of my dad. That was ringing in our minds all the time. Thinking about those names, and the fact that we were in Rwanda but we didn't have a total right to be there, and that there was no way to go back to Burundi because we didn't know any of our dad's relatives – all of this contributed to our pain and to the many questions on our minds.

I got the chance to go to secondary school, and to go to university. It was when I was at university that I received the message of healing and reconciliation, and it helped me so much, because it helped me to be with my wounds. I was healed from my wounds. But it also had a big impact on my mind: it renewed my mind. I had a strong prejudice against Tutsis, but the training helped me to celebrate diversity, to accept others, to see and understand that anyone is capable of doing bad things, whether Tutsi or Hutu. But if we come together and accept one another, we cultivate peace: we can live longer, and we can live in peace. I continued to be healed time after time, bit by bit. Healing is a process, and even now there are still some things to deal with, but you no longer have that hatred, and you cannot be driven to the wrong side. You have a good memory, a good mind. There is no longer that poison in your mind so that, if someone does wrong to you, you don't immediately start to say: "He's a Hutu. He's a Tutsi." No longer.

That's my story. One of the signs that I have been healed and renewed in my mind is that, when I started to date, I didn't have any criteria based on ethnicity. I loved, and I expressed my wish. And I thought: "Why am I loving a Tutsi? And what is attracting me to that Tutsi?" I am interested in her character, her personality. But I still hesitated. It took me two and a half years to give in to my wish to marry her. During that time, I was asking myself: "Am I serious? Am I able to live with someone to whom we did a wrong thing? Hutus killed her father, her mum, her brothers and sisters. Will I cope with the mourning period, when she is suffering, she is remembering?" I tried to love other girls, and thought: "Maybe I can love someone else." But it didn't happen. So I found that, maybe, I am serious. I can manage it.

I asked her to marry me and, after a few months, she responded positively, and now we have two children, and we work together here. At the moment, she is on maternity leave, because she gave birth last month. We have crises as others have crises, and we enjoy each other. We have a life like everyone else. There is nothing visible that is connected to ethnicity, to my background, or to her background. The history of Rwanda doesn't affect us in a negative way. When there is something wrong – maybe some political issue which is connected to the background of Rwanda, either on the Hutu side or the Tutsi side – we are not affected. We judge it as people who are healed, as people of the Holy Nation, as people who are Christian. So, we don't see any effect. We don't see it.

So, in brief, that is my story.

Many young people in Rwanda today were born after the genocide, or were very young during the genocide. What kind of messages do you think parents, teachers, and older people in

the community need to give to young people to help them understand that time?

Yes, children might even ask: "Where is our grandfather, our grandmother?" It is not easy because, in Rwanda, ethnicity is not something that is clear. It's not like in Uganda or Congo, where they have four hundred ethnic groups. In Rwanda, the ethnic groups we have are not scientifically true, because we speak the same language and we share the same culture. When you want to talk to a Hutu or a Tutsi you don't need a translator. Maybe we are from the same ancestor, I don't know. But the Hutu, Tutsi and the Twa were more like social classes, determined by wealth. Some were rich, others middle, others hunters, others farmers. But the problem was, during the colonial time, those things started to have ethnic connotations, and after independence, the government – the people who took power – polarised those things. Then people started to believe in those stereotypes about the Hutu, the Tutsi and the Twa, and they started to define the characteristics of each group.

So, in Rwanda today, it is hard to bring back those labels and to say: "These are the Tutsi, these are the Twa, these are the Hutu, so we have to live together." It is hard. But we just teach them to grow with a culture of peace. Also, we tell them: "Maybe you will hear about the history of your father, or your mother, or some of your relatives. That might be painful for you, but don't make the same mistake as your forefathers. Try to accept one another, and to understand one another. Try to have this culture of peace because that is what will sustain you. It is what will help you to live longer. Otherwise, you will fall into the same mistake as your forefathers."

It depends on their age. When you talk to people who are about 18 years old, you just bring the history as it was, and they are not confused by their so-called ethnicity. All of them know: "I am a Tutsi. I am a Twa. I am a Hutu." But we are prevented from talking about these things because of the government. The government is scared to let these things be openly talked about. But young people know, because there are associations of genocide survivors, so everyone can know who he is. So when they are around 18 to 20 years old, we bring the story as it was, and help them to see the root of the problem. The problem was prejudice. So we help them try to live a life without prejudice, because if you continue to emphasise this prejudice, the things that happened in 1994 will happen again. So: accept one another, celebrate diversity, and it will help you to live longer.

In brief, what we need to do for young people is to help them to grow in the culture of peace and to have the values of peace. As Christians, we tell them to have the values of the Holy Nation, where everyone is accepted without any bias: you are accepted just as you are, and you are the image of God, and you can portray unique characteristics of God that no-one else can portray. If we put all those things together, they can help us. We also teach them that, even if they're not accepted officially, our differences are our means to develop, to grow, to build our country. Because our differences are based, not on hatred or division, but on things that are good. If I am a farmer and you have cows, we can complement one another. We try to show them the wealth that we have in our diversity. It is the same with the political parties: they are diverse, but all of them have good elements. How can we put all those things together? We complement one another.

So, we try to teach them unity in diversity. That is our strength. That diversity is not a sin; it is not bad. Many people used to say: "To be Hutu, Twa, Tutsi – this is an evil thing." And we try to tell them: "It is not evil. It is evil because the devil tried to use it like that. But if you look deeply, you will see that it is a treasure."

And the focus of that is trust, that trust is the main factor in making social cohesion possible. Is that right?

In the context of Rwanda, it is. Because of the individualism that you find in other countries, trust is not really seen as the prevailing factor. It is at the same level as other factors. But, in Rwanda, trust is the major measurement of social cohesion, because in Rwanda there is this particular case where neighbours killed neighbours, and today they live together. That is a problem. If I am a survivor, how can I trust that this man will not do it again? Or, how can he trust me that I will not seek revenge? If I give him my daughter to be married to his son, how can I trust this relationship? So, trust in Rwanda is something very, very important to address, because we don't even talk about our ethnicity openly. It is something we hide in our hearts, and it is something we have in our minds, and we leave it there. It is like wearing invisible glasses. I know that I am going to that office, or I am going to that village, and I try to scan all the people who are there through my glasses. Or I can live in that house, but I cannot live in this one. If I go there, I have to speak in this way...and so on. We are all treating each other like this because we don't have trust. So trust is very important for social cohesion.

What's your main role with Mercy Ministries now? What kind of things are you involved with at the moment?

At the moment, I'm involved in running schools. We have schools of reconciliation – both national and international. On the national level, I run it. On the international level, there is a partnership with Le Rucher Ministries. I am a technical person for that: pricing, trying to organise logistics, things like that. In the school, we give the message of reconciliation in an organised package. It is a school that runs for 22 days, in three parts. There is the part of healing the wounds of ethnic conflict, where we bring people through the workshop, to heal themselves, and afterwards we give them training so that they can then run the ministry of healing and reconciliation. After that, they do practical work. We bring them into the community, to teach, to be familiar with the material, and we try to coach them. Then there is peace-building and community outreach. We have the message of peace, but what can we do with it? So, we can help vulnerable people, marginalised people, with training, constructing improved stoves, kitchens, or gardens, but always accompanying the message of peace. They interact with people in that context of peace.

Afterwards, there is a kind of leadership training, helping people to see how they can work together. Normally, we suggest people work as a group because it is a demanding ministry. The way you can minister is not the way I can minister. For example, if we have a workshop and there is a woman who is crying, maybe I am not the right person to go and comfort her; maybe a woman should go to comfort her. Or, my testimony might be relevant to one side of the group, and yours can complement it for the other group. So, we want to complement one another, so that people can have this message in its inclusiveness. As a group, we try to show how to work together – team dynamic, communication, character, integrity – so that they minister while being healthy, and having healthy relationships with God and with people.

Tell me about the Reconciliation Lighthouse.

We have a database of reconciliation organisations, and we have collected information from those organisations, including their approach, their target group, and the challenges they are facing – a snapshot of information about them. The purpose of that database is to help people who want to do research, or to visit, or to experience one of the approaches. If they are here, we can help them to contact those organisations.

The second part is an artistic showcase: we have pictures, and those pictures form stations. It is a path interrupted by stations, and each station has its own message. It is a kind of summary of the "Healing the Wounds of Ethnic Conflict" message. For example, the first station is celebrating diversity, and it is a summary of one of the topics we have in the book of HWEC. There is also a bit about prejudice, and a wounded heart. We try to show the offender and the offended person that they are bound; they are together. After the crime of the killing, no-one lives alone: in their mind, their memory, they live together with the offender. They are together. So we try to show how you behave, and how you relate to other people, when you are wounded. What are the effects? After that, there is a healing station, where we talk about the power of the cross: that the cross is there to help us to be healed. Then comes the part of reconciliation where we see forgiveness, repentance, and standing in the gap, where you can confess on behalf of your group. Then we go to the other station, which is the Holy Nation, where we celebrate our diversity: we value everyone and we affirm one another. From this we can have a vision; we can contribute to the same vision with different backgrounds. So that is the Reconciliation Lighthouse. This helps us to speak to a mass of people in a short time.

Who made the pictures for the different stations?

We had a workshop on Healing the Wounds of Ethnic Conflict, for artists. Some were painters, others were dancers, others were writers. So after the workshop, we told them: "Try to write down some inspiration from this workshop." And the artists came up with that lighthouse. And when we saw the pictures and the explanations, we found what we wanted. We had had this idea of the lighthouse but we didn't know exactly what it would be like. It was like a journey that reflects the journey of healing, but what would it look like? After the workshop, those people came up with those pictures and they portrayed exactly what we wanted. Then we called them back and told them: "Do those things." We tried to give some comments and they made improvements, and then they came up with those.

How do people hear about the Reconciliation Lighthouse? How do they get involved in that?

We do mobilisations. Normally, we partner with churches and other organisations that are involved in the area of reconciliation. We send flyers. We also go and talk to them, and they select people, and they send delegates. The national one is difficult. It is not easy to get people to come, because the Rwandan reconciliation does not sit well in the ear of normal people, so we try to show them the importance of this training. Some come, and they are the ones who, when they go back to their homes, will mobilise other people: "I went to a place and I have seen this thing. It is very, very good and you should go." This material is very powerful because it doesn't address only this issue of ethnicity. You can see the wholeness in it. You will see some people saying: "Oh, this material helped me to live very well with my wife," even though we didn't teach about family relationships. And someone might say: "I am now managing my subordinate very well, because of this material." So it is something that makes you think about your personality, and how we have to live with people in a peaceful way. It ministers to different aspects of life.

But for the international one, it is easy. We contact other big organisations and they start to circulate the flyers, and people can apply. They can also use the Le Rucher website. Many people used to visit that website, and they apply. Now, we can count eighteen countries that have attended this school, all over the world, including countries which are very, very far away; like Afghanistan, Nepal, Myanmar. We realised: "Oh, this material can help the world."

GAUDENCE

Could you tell me about how and why you got involved with HWEC, and how the workshops helped you?

I am a Hutu, and after the genocide we fled to Congo, and we lived in a refugee camp. Then, afterwards, we came back to Rwanda and my father was put in prison, accused of being involved in the genocide. In my heart, I hated Tutsis so much because they put my father in prison.

I lived with that anger for so long because I would always take food to my father – always, every day – and my heart was so broken because of that. Later, I was invited to a HWEC workshop.

When I came to the workshop, in the introduction they told us about the bitter roots of prejudice, and they came to the point of our own history of Rwanda: ethnicity. They talked about ethnicity. And when they arrived at that topic of bitter roots, I discovered that even I, myself, had that bitter root, because I hated Tutsis so much. When they reached the topic of forgiveness, I started crying so much because I realised how much I was wounded by the fact that my father was put in prison because of Tutsis, and I found that I had that hatred for the Tutsi.

When we arrived at the Cross Workshop, we held each other's hands, and it was time for the part of the workshop when you write all your pain and wounds down and you burn them. When we reached that point, I cried so much, because it was very touching for me. I was together with a person called Japheth. We were in the same choir, but I hated him so much because he was a Tutsi. At that time, I went and embraced him, saying, "I used to hate you because of who you were, but now I feel that I forgive you."

After reconciling with him, I felt something falling down, falling off my heart, and I felt released. I realised that all Tutsis are not bad, and that on both sides – Tutsi and Hutu – there are good and bad people. Before, I had some prejudice that all Tutsis are bad, but after this workshop, I realised that everyone is good or bad on his own side.

After the workshop, I committed myself to go and teach my mum about what I had taken away from the workshop. Before this, every time I was reminded that my father was in prison, I would throw down everything that I had in my hand and say: "Oh, this is typical Tutsi!" But after the workshop, I committed to go and testify to my mother and to tell her what had happened to me. Because she, also, would relate every pain that she had in that time to the Tutsi. She would say: "All this is because of the Tutsi." Later, my mother was also released, and now she is ok.

So, now I am going to talk about how I benefitted from the workshop, and how God has redeemed all my pain.

After the workshop, I committed to be one of the people who will also build reconciliation.

In that time, they were planning for a workshop in a northern province. It's a place called Byumba. They were planning a workshop there, and I didn't know much about the people who would go there, but I heard a voice telling me to be prepared, and that I would be among the people who would go.

Joseph was one of the people who was training us in that workshop, and God had told me before that He would do something special through that training. Later, we got into small groups to share our pains, and in those small groups we were sharing our pains and giving prayer requests to each other, and we were together with two men: one was from eastern province, and the other was from western province. When we were sharing our pains, I shared with them how I have this zeal to work for this ministry of healing and reconciliation but I was responsible for my young sisters, and I was wondering how I could be involved in this ministry, and who would stay at home with those kids. During that time of sharing, we each had to pray for one another, and when the pastor from eastern province was laying his hand on me, praying for me, I heard a voice saying: "I give you a new father."

The man that I was talking about is Mugasa Joseph. He is also involved in this ministry, and he pastored so many people in the eastern province. When I heard that voice, saying, "Now, I give you a new father," I cried and I said, "How can this be happening?" Because he is a Tutsi. It was very hard to receive that message. Then we went back to the room, and someone came to me and told me, "Just confess the new hope that is in you." So then I told them my testimony that, before coming to the workshop, I had heard a voice saying, "I want to do something new for you," and then, when we were praying, that I heard a voice saying that now I am given a new father. From that time, I confessed that Mugasa Joseph, is now my father. It was very good for me.

After confessing that, Mugasa Joseph, who was just a little way away, came running, and we embraced each other, and then I cried so much, because when I was happy I used to cry. Then I wondered, "How can it be, Father, that out of the hate that I had for Tutsi, you have now given me a Tutsi father?" Later, I went to his home and I was like one of his children, and I received all the love that you can receive from a father, and it was very touching for me to realise that now I have a Tutsi father.

I experienced how much God redeemed this horror. Because at that time I was single, and the time came for me to get married, and that family, they were like my real father and mother. I remember how the mother took care of me, sending me messages: "How are you doing?" Helping me. They are the ones who were responsible for every part of my wedding ceremony, everything. That was my family. I experienced love there, and I really felt how God redeemed my sorrow. I realised that it's only at the cross that people of different ethnic groups can meet and become one, and from that time I just committed myself to be the one who gives that message of healing and reconciliation. I want to testify to the other Rwandese that it is God who really redeems our pain and sorrow.

That was my story. Thank-you so much.

Thank-you so much for sharing it. It's an amazing story. Do you, in your community, feel that there are still lots of people who feel the way that you used to feel?

There are.

And do you do reconciliation work in your community?

Yes, I do.

What kinds of things do you do? How do you share what you received at the workshops, and what you received at the cross?

I use different approaches. One is a formal training workshop, and also through songs of healing and reconciliation. Also personal dialogues, conversation, where you sit with a person and you listen to him or her. Also, helping people during the national mourning period: I used to help people who are traumatised, or who have other issues.

How is it for children who have been born since the genocide? What kinds of messages do they need to hear?

I think they need to be told the true history of Rwanda, but emphasising how bad the experience was. That new generation has to rebuild our country, and not based on that bad history or experience.

What would you say to someone who felt that they wouldn't be able to forgive because what happened to them is too painful; it was too bad to forgive?

We don't force him or her to forgive, because I know that it is not easy to forgive, and forgiveness is a process. It is not the kind of thing that you can just do immediately. But what we do, without forcing him to forgive, is to show him how painful it is not to forgive, how you are tied to the other person. It is like you are together with the person who offended you. And we tell him how it can also bring death, because of that pain. We don't focus on telling him to forgive but we show him how painful it is to remain with that kind of pain, and we tell him that it is a process. After a time, when people realise that it is real, that it is true, they forgive. They commit themselves to forgive, without being forced.

When you first went to a workshop, did you hear people talking from the other side about hatred for Hutu? And how did that make you feel?

In the workshops, when I hear different people sharing those kind of ideas, I feel that it is their experience, and it is based on their history, and my intention there, or my burden, or my passion, is to help those people to get released from those bad thoughts, or those identities. It is like an identity that they put on one ethnicity. My passion is just to help them remove that false identity, and show them the true identity: that we are all the same.

How do you feel your life is different now to how it was before you were released from the pain and the hatred you felt towards Tutsi?

Now, I feel joy and love to receive everyone in his ethnicity; either the person that I can see obviously is a Tutsi, or another Hutu. Now

I feel that I am free, and I am open to talking to everyone, without hesitating and thinking, "Who is that person?" Now I feel that I am free to talk to anyone, no matter who he is, whether he is a Tutsi or a Hutu. I feel free and open to everyone, no matter who he is. I feel that we are all one; we are from one Father, and we are all one.

Do you think a lot of people still carry a certain mistrust around with them?

Yes, this is the life that we live, that everyone lives. We used to confess things that are not in our hearts, showing people that we live in peace and there is no problem; yet we have pain in our hearts, and what we confess is not what is in our hearts. So that's true of many people, because when a person is not healed emotionally, or in their heart, it is not easy to show who he really is. We used to cover up, to show that we are ok, we are fine, yet in our hearts we have that pain.

So we need to be healed in our hearts before that then becomes how we relate to other people, and forgive other people.

How do you think the work of HWEC could be used, and can be powerful, for people outside of Rwanda, or outside of this immediate context?

I think that other countries can learn from Rwanda by hearing the experience that we went through, and how we came to reconcile with each other. They can learn from different programmes that we have in Rwanda, like Gacaca, and other programmes that put people back together. I think they can learn from us, and here they have a good lesson to follow.

Were you involved in Gacaca at all? How do you think that has helped people? What was the value of that?

For me, the good thing that I saw in Gacaca is when people would just sit down, and people were free to tell the whole truth. One person could rise and say, "I am the one who killed your family," before any person accused him or her. Those cases when people could just confess, without other people accusing him. It helped some people to be released, hearing a person confessing the bad things that he had done to them. Some people were released, and they forgave each other, and that was a good experience because it released people, it reconciled people. From that Gacaca court, many people – many Tutsi and Hutu – reconciled to the level that they can marry each other: Hutu can marry a Tutsi and Tutsi can marry a Hutu, because of that kind of justice, and the truth that they confessed.

And there's release on both sides, isn't there?

Thank-you so much for sharing your story with me; it's really encouraging and inspiring to hear it.

DAVID

I'm happy to share my story because I think it could help somebody I never even meet.

I will not say too much about before the genocide because our history was good, the family was together, so there were not many problems. My life was easy because I was so young.

I was born in February '86.

When the genocide happened, I wasn't with my father and my mum. I was at my uncle's, my mother's brother. I was visiting him. I think the genocide started on a Wednesday and I was supposed to go back home on the Thursday, but because the genocide happened I had to stay where I was, because it was about 8 km to get home. So I stayed there with him. I was also with my brother, Janvier. I didn't get too much trouble because I was too young. At that point, the killing was not concerned with children. At the start, the killings only concerned the men. Even women were not killed. But the day after, and the day after, they started to kill everyone. The only reason to be killed was that you were a Tutsi, and you know the history. The only crime was being a Tutsi, so being a Tutsi was equal to being killed. No other reason.

I remember, one week later, we went to the Catholic church, which is called Sainte-Famille. We spent about two months there. The killers would come into the church to take people, and then go and kill them outside. Even then, I didn't feel directly troubled or shocked, because the killing was happening outside the church and I was inside. After that, I went to another place, which was taken by the RPF. That place is around Masaka; it's called Kawouga.

I knew that my father was dead after the genocide. I met my mum in June, and she told me that my father had died. But because I was too young, I didn't even react straight away. It was only later that I fully realised that my dad had died. When I started at school, seeing my mum struggling and searching through our things, that is when I realised that there was someone missing in our family. It was at that time that I started doing small jobs: selling things in the markets, finding ways to make money myself, thinking about how I could survive and how I could help my mum.

My story started in secondary school, because that is where I learned about the genocide. I participated in survivors' associations, which lead me to realise that I am a Tutsi so I have to live with the Tutsi only, and not with Hutus. Survivors' associations had three parts: the association members, the honoured members, and anyone who was interested in supporting or living with the survivors. I took hold of only one part: the members who are Tutsi. So I had to live with them. I even paid a lot to uncover people's personal identity, to find out if there were people hidden amongst us who were not Tutsi. I was the father of the family, and I was forcing too much energy into building that sense of ethnicity, and growing that hatred.

I was becoming someone else. Even if I could talk and laugh with you, I would still look at you and see that you are not my friend, or you are not someone to talk to, or not someone to deal with, even if we were in the same group or the same choir. Our choir was Christian, and my mum was a Christian, and my mum taught me that we don't have to hate people. But I learned something different at the secondary school: I learned that I have to be a Tutsi. I am a survivor, and the Hutus killed my father, even though I wasn't with him. So that grew up in me.

Coming back to my sister's story, and me: I think I was in senior 4 when I started to realise that there were some people who were trying to come into our life, and they were Hutus. I didn't handle it well, because if you are hating people, you are hating, and nothing can push you to love. Nothing can push you to love someone you don't have to love. I was like that person: "I don't have to love Hutus because they are not even Rwandans." I even told my friend in secondary school: "If I could get a gun, I would kill the person who killed my dad. I will kill him." I didn't know him, and maybe I would never see him, but if I could find him I would kill him.

The hatred was growing up in me. You couldn't see that I was not a Christian. You couldn't see that I was hating people, because I was laughing with everyone, I was talking to everyone, but inside I could not talk about deeper things with the Hutu people. Most of the friends I had were Tutsi, but I also had Hutu guys in the same group, and I would act like I loved them and that I didn't care. But I did care. I cared about what was inside me.

It was at my sister's wedding that people realised that I was a different person to the one they had known. I refused to even go to the wedding because her husband is Hutu. I started a fight: "You don't have to love him, you don't have to go to him. Please... You didn't even participate in the survivors' association, you don't know what happened..." And she was telling me: "From my side, I've forgiven. I've not even cared. Love just pushed me to go there." I didn't go to her wedding. I was busy. Because I was a photographer, I was hired by someone else as an excuse to miss her wedding.

After that, I didn't even feel that I could go to visit her because she got married to a Hutu: "I will never go to her house. I will never." But it is in my character that I love children, so once her baby came, I started to imagine how I would take care of that baby, how I would hold that baby; because I loved her, I loved the baby, but I didn't love the father. Love grew slowly, slowly – but for the baby, not for the father. The baby was loving me too much. Even during the night, the baby would stand up, crying, and saying: "Daddy, Dad-didet." She called me "Dad-didet". She has too much love for me.

When I went to the healing and reconciliation sessions with Mercy Ministries, that is when I started to realise that I was wrong. Even though I was Christian, I was wrong, because I was not really a Christian. After one week I started to think, within me, that I had to ask for forgiveness from the right person: my sister's husband. I think it was one day before we ended the workshop, we had a session about asking for forgiveness. Some people were Hutu and they asked for forgiveness for the things they had done wrong: they killed people, so they could stand in the gap. Someone told me: "Someone who's Tutsi can come and hug me, and that will be a sign that I am forgiven by Tutsis." So I did that, but afterwards I realised that I still didn't like them. I was hugging him because I felt obliged to do that because I'm Tutsi, but I didn't love him really. I think it was Omer, who is a member of staff for Mercy Ministries.

After that, my heart started to tell me: "Because you hate them, you also have to ask for forgiveness." And I was 100% convinced that I had to tell my sister's husband; I had to say that I had hated him too much. I called him, asking him for forgiveness. He was the one I really hated because he took my sister, and it seemed to me that he didn't have to take her. This is where the hating came from. But even the other Hutus, I could not pretend that I really felt love for them in my heart.

So I asked for forgiveness, because of the Mercy Ministries workshop. I even told Joseph: "Your ministry made me appreciate the cross." This was the only sin I could not speak about, or show to people. It was inside my heart. So I asked for forgiveness, and I have been forgiven. Glory to the Lord! From that moment, I am being honest; I am not lying, or giving this testimony to show people that honest people are Christian. From that time, I realised that I was wrong. I cried a lot because I thought: "I didn't go to my sister's wedding because of that hatred." But I did something that was a significant sign. In our culture, a brother gives his sister to a man to be married, so during the wedding I was supposed to give my sister to her husband, but I was not there. I don't know what happened on the day. But even though the wedding had already happened, even though they are already husband and wife, I took the initiative to give my sister to her husband as a sign that I am participating in the wedding, even though it has already happened. When I realised that I was wrong, I did that: we took hands, and gave her to her husband, as a sign, and to finally fulfil my role.

From that moment I can truly say that I am free. I can share, I can talk, I can be friendly to anyone; even the people I work with. I work at the memorial, and sometimes I tell them, "We have to forgive." And they say, "That is a political issue, and we are in real life. Can you really forgive, in real life?" And I say, "I did. I've forgiven. And they forgive me because I hated them. So I've forgiven them, and they also have forgiven me. Before, there were things that separated us…" and they find it hard to understand: "You, David? You forgave?" Yes, I did. I live with everyone. But I cannot say that it's an easy thing. It requires training, conversations, and the Spirit of

God to be released from a hardened spirit, but it's a process. Even though I'm saved, there are other people who are not. It's a process to go through, and we're still in that process. We're still telling people to be reconciled. The government of Rwanda has focussed on reconciling, but in reality there is not true reconciliation, in people's hearts. Within our groups and with our friends we can talk and we can share, but inside, people know that they don't like each other, because of the history.

When did you take part in the workshop?

It was May last year – 2014 – at Mercy Ministries. It was within the songwriting workshop. During the morning we wrote songs, then in the afternoon we had training in reconciliation.

How do you think the music, the songs, and the songwriting help people get to the point of reconciliation?

I think the main thing that people can relate to, and that brings people together, is music. I don't think anyone dislikes music. Even if you don't love it, you still listen to music, for reflective time. So I think passing the message through music will help many people, because they will listen to the music attentively, and carefully. There are people who don't like to talk, or to negotiate with words, but if you pass the message through music, he might listen alone and think, "Wow. They are talking to me. Even though they are not in front of me, they are talking to me."

So music will help a lot. I think the results will not be clear immediately, but people could be saved through the music. For example, during the course that we had at Serena, I shared my testimony for three to five minutes, and people said, "Oh, is that the same person? Is that the guy we knew before? Is that David?" Because they knew that I didn't come to the wedding, and I was 100% sure that I wasn't going to go. So people listen to that and say, "Wow. I can't imagine that Jesus could save David. He was born in the church, he grew up in the church, and then, after 20-something years, he realised that he made a mistake."

So through music, or concerts, people start to notice that something has happened, and it helps them to realise that they, themselves, could also change.

After the concert, two people called me and asked, "Can we please record your testimony?" And I told them, "I'm available. Whenever you want me, I can come." One man told me that he was a journalist, and he said, "I want to ask your permission to record your message as a video, then share it on TV," because he worked for a private TV company. I told him, "Yes, I'm free. You just come and we'll talk." And he said, "Tell me, really – I'm on the phone, but I'm not recording – have you really forgiven? Are you really reconciled?"

He still wouldn't believe you.

"You really did that, within your heart?" And I told him, "Yes, I did. You can't know that I am telling the truth, but I know that it's the truth: I've been saved. I've been saved, 100%. I'm not hating anyone. I've been saved." He told me, "I'm not sure, because I know you." But I said, "Maybe the time will come when you will realise that I was saved."

My wife knows that the thing that has really discouraged me, or that is so sad to me, is that I didn't attend my sister's wedding, and she is the only sister I have. My wife knows that I can say, "I was wrong, I was wrong." She also told me, "You have to ask for forgiveness." She is the only person who told me that. Other people say, "You were right. You were right. You can't change the history of a country. You can do nothing to change it." And I say, "No, I have to. I have to." I have even thought about how and why we can do something for the youth, to change their minds. Because, even if you're born after the genocide, these things must affect you as you grow up; I don't know what it must be like for them. There was a nine-year-old child who told his friends at school, "If you come and kill my mum, I will take a machete and kill you, like the people in '94." Even though he was not involved – he was not even born – there are things in people's minds.

I think, by sharing testimonies, by creating songs that talk about reconciliation, by going to the preparations, people in the cities – or the whole country – will start to know that they have to reconcile. It is good that the government has removed the ethnic identities on our ID, and maybe that is a start, but we can continue this through songs, and through worship, telling people that God doesn't like this division. Some people appear to be reconciled because of the political line: we have to live together. The RPF statements created this policy. But by starting there, people could even go to another, deeper level of being reconciled in their hearts and their minds.

Because that's a whole other step, actually being reconciled in your heart.

Yes. At the moment, you can't show someone that you hate him because he's a Hutu or he's a Tutsi. You might even go to prison, because the laws condemn you. But, for the moment they live together: "You are Hutu. I'm hating you but I'm not telling you that. It's on my mind but I'm not telling you." This is because of the government statements: "You are Rwandan. You are no longer Hutu, you are longer Tutsi, you are no longer Twa. You are Rwandan." Even as I'm telling you that I'm Tutsi, I'm starting to think: "What am I saying?" because the government has told us: "You are not a Tutsi. You are Rwandan." Even though I'm saying it in a testimony, something triggers in my mind: "Oh! No longer. You are no longer a Tutsi." Because of the government statements. But, in my mind, I know that I am a Tutsi, and I can know that someone else is a Hutu.

So, at the moment, they are living together but they are not forgiven; they are not reconciled. There are some people who are really reconciled, who have had a chance to do the workshops, for example. Some people are able to say, "I forgive all of the people who have killed my family. I will not even claim for the assets, for the damages. I forgive you." But the majority are living together but not forgiving, not reconciled. This is the big percentage. You can't know exactly who is on this side or who is on that side, but I think the gospel, the message of God, is the only way to change people's minds; because the hating is now in the mind rather than being outwardly obvious.

Do you think that most people don't see this hating as a problem, even now? Or do you think people know, on one level, that they are not truly reconciled?

When you are not reconciled, you know by yourself. And once you're reconciled, once you're saved, you also notice that by yourself. Let us take an example of doing business, or sharing something that can bring some income: people don't care that you are Tutsi or Hutu, they just share and work together to build a business. But sometimes there is a limit, and someone says, "I cannot trust this person 100%." There are certain limits, and they know that they are not reconciled. Maybe they don't know what to do about it: "What can I do to come up through this hatred, to a place where I can be reconciled?" They try to respect the government's needs, but maybe they are really thinking, "I want to reconcile." Maybe. Maybe there are some people who want to reconcile, but who don't know how to take the first step. So they need someone else, with a new strategy, because most of the possible strategies have been tried: "You need to be reconciled. Please live together. We are Rwandans." Maybe they need something else to motivate them to come up and out of that hatred.

Do you feel like it would be more helpful for people to be able to talk about it more?

I think, the truth is, when you don't have a response to something, it's better to leave it. This is what the government did: "We don't have a response to this. We don't have an exact way to reconcile people. Better to tell them that, 'You are all Rwandans'." This is what the government did. The situation in Rwanda is different from that of Burundi. In Burundi, they still have those words: "You are Hutu and I'm Tutsi. I don't have to live with you." But in Rwanda, they have tried to go beyond that. But you might have known your neighbour for 20 years and you know that he is a Tutsi. You can't just forget that and say, "He is not a Tutsi. He is a Rwandan." The process of convincing people has been missed. So, from their point of view, they say: "Let us tell them that they are all Rwandans." This was the reason: to go beyond, or to pass through. "You are just Rwandan. Don't think about what is down here, what is inside you, just pass through the problems, pass through the ethnicity." But this only gives a response to half of the problem. Our president has a problem, because if all Rwandans live in peace, every person is focussing on a business, and on life, rather than focussing on ethnicity. But in Burundi, they go together. You are doing business, but you are Tutsi. You are going on the bus but you are a Tutsi, so I don't have to come with you on the bus. Why? I have to take my bus. This is the situation.

For Rwanda, it served only a part of the problem. You can't kill people, accusing them of being a Hutu or a Tutsi, so you find another way of killing him: maybe he took your assets, maybe he took something else that belonged to you. But the problem doesn't come down to ethnicity. It is really necessary to talk about it. Let us take an example – even though I don't wish it to happen again in Rwanda – let us take an example of someone who might win an election, who is not Kagame, and they say, "I'm bringing back ethnic IDs." This will bring us back to 1995 or 1996, when people wanted revenge. Imagine if someone brings back this idea: it might make you realise that you have not been reconciled, you have not got past this problem.

This situation deals with the hating by just calming people down. It is like saying to people, "Just calm down. You lost something, you lost your relative, but calm down. Don't think about it. He's dead. He's passed away. You will never see him. Just calm down. Just continue, continue." But teenagers started to realise that we had really lost someone, as happened to me: I realised that my dad had passed away. In 1997-1998, I started struggling. And this is the same case. 15 years or 100 years later, this problem can come back: "Oh! You killed us in 1994. We are in 2020 and we have to kill you back, because it is our turn to kill you."

Because we passed through the problems; we didn't go too deeply into them and talk about it. We didn't want to know the source, the cause, whose fault it was, or how we could have fought against it. So, from my point of view – even though I'm not a politician – it is better to talk about it. It is better to go deeper, and to know what the reason was, even before '59. Because the history tells us that being a Tutsi meant that you had two cows, and being a Hutu meant you were someone else, and being a Twa was another group. From there, we can ask, "So, what changed?" And we talk about it. "After this, what happened?" And we talk about it. What has an impact? What is necessary? Is it good, or can we leave it behind? This is what we need. But I don't think the politicians will go through this. The only thing that can make people go through this is to go through the gospel: tell them that you have to repent. It's a sin, just like other sins. If you say that to someone who doesn't even believe in Jesus, who doesn't believe in the Lord, he will tell you, "Ah, that's just for pastors." But if he listens once, five times, ten times, he will start to realise that it is reconciling.

This child of nine years old was born after the genocide, but he knew that he would kill someone if they killed his mum. So it comes back, always. But if you don't hide a story, and you speak the truth of the story, people start to see that it was about the past, it was about division. The injuries were not for us; it was about the people who brought this attitude with them. We cannot say, "The Belgians brought this idea because of colonisation" because then we will start to have conflict between two countries. But I think there is a sense of creating a conversation, going deeply into it, and not just saying, "You brought it." Not just accusing someone, saying, "You did it. You did it." No, just sharing what is necessary to share, and coming up with a solution that could save the whole population of the country; maybe even the whole of East Africa. Because this begins in

Rwanda, and spreads to Burundi, and it has started to go to Kenya. So, if we pass through, it will even spread out to the whole world. Even the Jews could say, "Oh! We have to kill the Germans because they were the source of the Holocaust." But it's better to talk, and to go deeply into what happened. But no politician will tell you that is good.

Our politicians will say: "The reconciliation has been 100% successful. We are reconciled." It is their objective to show the world – the UN, the sponsors – that we have reconciled. But being 100% reconciled means there is no-one in prison because they are forgiven. This is the real sense of being reconciled. If you are reconciled with someone, you can go to the prison – or to the government, or the court – and say, "I have forgiven that person. He is in prison because of me, but I release him of his sin, so he may now come out of prison." But we have a lot of people who are still in prison because of the killings. Even if you say you have forgiven that person, they might still be in prison for the rest of their life: they can't come back into society and live with you, and share lunch with you as we are sharing lunch now. Let's take the example of when black and white people could not sit at the same table and share lunch: there was a table for the white people and a table for the black people. But because of new ideas and understanding, we are now one, and we have no reason to hate a person who doesn't deserve hate. So this is why we are sharing together, but this could not have happened before. This is the real image of being reconciled. You could even go to visit the person who killed your dad and take lunch to him: "Please, eat, because I have forgiven you."

But because we are just passing through, there are people in prison who have been baptised with that sin, who have not been forgiven. Maybe the president can forgive them, because it is a time for forgiveness. On the political side, he can forgive people. He has done that twice already: about nine people came out of prison because of his forgiveness. But we have to do our part. We have to say, "We've forgiven them. Please release them, because they have been forgiven." But this, I think, cannot happen because, on the political side, we are saying that we are reconciled. But if we go deeply into the history, we can come up with a solution. On the political side, they don't agree. They say, "This is not a solution. You're bringing trouble. You're bringing us back, and we don't want it. We are in 2020. We have a project. We have to show the people that we have been reconciled. We have to show the people that we have come up with new plans, and that we are developing ourselves as a country. So you can't say that we are no longer reconciled because the UN will ask, 'Why did you say, before, that you were reconciled?'"

I cannot even blame them because they are dealing with big things.

From the political point of view, as you said, if they don't have a response then the only real option for them is to say: "We are all Rwandans!"

Yes: "We are Rwandans. We are Rwandans." But for Christian people, it is our time to say that we are Rwandans, but we are Rwandans who are not reconciled. They have to agree that, "You are Rwandan but you are not reconciled yet with your neighbour, or with someone who you need to be reconciled with." This is the only remaining way: to go through the gospel, sing about reconciliation, talk about reconciliation, through the Bible, through the gospel, through songs. Then people will get to know: "We were wrong the last time."

JANVIÈRE

After the genocide, I hated the Hutu because I loved my father and they killed him. My father was dear to me. I was the first-born and the only girl, with four brothers. I think, in Rwanda, fathers have a special love for their daughters. After the genocide, I hated the Hutu and I had decided to join the army, to kill the Hutu. Our parents didn't tell us about ethnic groups. We went to church to sing and pray, and so on. But when I was in secondary school, it was there that this message was preached to me. When I was preparing to join the army, it was at that time that I went to the Mercy Ministries seminar. It was in that workshop that I was healed. But it was only me. He [David] still had hate. He was angry. But I was thinking, my mother is Christian, and she does not have ethnic groups in her mind.

After being healed, even though I received many declarations of love from different young men, I loved Gilbert. He's from a Hutu background. My husband is a Hutu. It was very hard to get engaged, because my mother refused, as well as my brothers, the whole of my large family, my friends, and even some of my church. So it was very hard for me. We waited almost seven years for the agreement from the government at the district level, and then my church, to be allowed to start the marriage process. Afterwards, I was living out my marriage without my family, just with some church members and a few friends. It was hard for me. I was feeling a lot of pain, because my mother was also my close friend. To be in the marriage without my mother and my brother was painful for me.

Later, I was praying and I shared my pain with Joseph, with our staff, and they prayed with me. After that, I proclaimed forgiveness to my mother. She refused. But later, she was sick for a long time. When I was pregnant, it the last evening at the hospital as I was preparing to give birth, and that was the time when my mother managed to greet my husband: in seven years of engagement and two years of marriage, that had never happened.

The next four days after giving birth to our lovely first-born daughter, my mother came to our home from the hospital holding our daughter, which was a cultural sign of blessing. That was the starting point of our restored relationship, and she continues to visit and talk to both of us! But later, she was sick for a long time. The last day we visited her at home, even though she was very sick, she was really happy to be with our daughter and she took time to proclaim blessings to my husband.

Where did you meet Gilbert?

We sing together in the choral choir.

David: Gilbert was the master, and she was assisting him. Maybe through that working relationship, something else was born!

It's interesting how one of the things that brought your family back together was you having a baby. It's quite powerful how that affected your relationships. What is she called?

J: Mercy. She is three years and seven months, I think.

D: I think that baby came to reconcile our families. She's the only one who pushed me to visit my sister's family. They got married in November, I think, and I just passed by her house once at Christmas. So I saw her home one month after the wedding, and then I passed about two years without going back. I remember one day, when my other brothers were there, she called me on the phone and said to me, "Please, come to my house. Please come."

So you went to the Mercy Ministries seminar. Was that before you had met Gilbert?

J: Yes, in '98.

Had you [David] had any interaction with Mercy Ministries before last year?

D: No, I didn't. I went to that workshop for the first time this last year.

How did you get involved with the choir?

D: My sister was in the choir, and I was leaving the children's choir. Once you're baptised, you go out from the children's choir and you choose one of the other choirs, where you can continue in worship. So I went straight to Amahoro Choir and joined my sister.

Was that how you got involved with Mercy Ministries?

D: It was before that. I joined the choir in 2000, but the workshop with Mercy Ministries happened some years later.

Do you think "Rabagirana, Rwanda" [the children's album] impacted you at all, or do you think it was still difficult because you didn't really understand your feelings completely, at that time?

D: No, for "Rabagirana, Rwanda" it was just singing. My mum called me at home and said, "We are launching an album for the children. Please will you come?" "Yes, I will." It was in the holidays, so I went. I didn't even realise what I was singing. It was just for children. I was about 10 or 12 years old. I was absent-minded, just singing. But the workshop that happened later was helpful for me.

I'm the master of the choir now; I have replaced Gilbert. The members of the choir knew me before, and they say, "How could you live with Gilbert, under his roof?" And I say, "I've forgiven. I love him!" After the workshop, I gave them my testimony, about how I've been healed, and the whole process, and they said, "Hey, this really happened!" They even wanted to go to Mercy Ministries, to have the same workshop, because they believed. They told me, "You were our master but we knew that you hated Hutus. We knew."

They knew you. They could tell.

D: Yes, they knew. I hated my sister's husband as he's from a Hutu background, so I was automatically on the side of those who were hating others from that historical "ethnic group". They told me, "We are aware that you are not a friend of ours. You're laughing with us, but you don't like us." But after that, I said, "Now, you are my friends. You are all my friends." And they told me, "Really, we have to go to that training. We have to go to the workshop, because something happened. Maybe the Holy Spirit came up." We went there as a group of 25 to 30 people, out of a choir of about 120, so it was only a minority that was able to go because of the budget. But I think, this year, the whole choir has to do that workshop, because it will help us to sing from our hearts. One of the songs that I was the main singer for had the lyrics: "Forgive me Lord. I've killed people. I've killed your children. I've taken back your fortune ...", and it is evidence of the transformation in me that, since I attended the workshop, something changed within me and I am now able to stand in the place of someone else.

I remember when we started to practise those songs, the words were too hard. The choir members who hadn't had the chance to experience the workshop didn't like the songs, and they said, "No, we cannot imagine how we can sing this song 'We killed people'? No, we didn't kill people. Why do you want us to sing that we killed people?" And we told them, "You just put yourself in the place of someone who did it, who doesn't have a chance to sing it. You just be that person. Imagine that you are in prison; imagine that you are giving a testimony that you have killed some people in the genocide." Some of my fellow singers refused to take that verse, but that is the verse that I sang in the big concert at Serena Hotel. The verse said, "Please, brothers, forgive me. I killed your daughters. I took back your cows, your fortune. I don't have any excuse. Please forgive me." Some people refused to sing it, but I stood up and said, "Even though this verse doesn't seem to concern me, I am ready to help others to vocalise and give a name or meaning to what is inside their hearts, as it is so difficult to find the courage to let it out."

So we started to realise how much every member of the choir needs the workshop. They need to be trained, they need to get informed, to get involved in what happened. What is healing? What is reconciliation? What is the process? How can I forgive? I was amazed to hear some fellow choir members from a Hutu background starting to say, "He is singing on our behalf. We are from this historically Hutu ethnic group, so this song's for us." What can we say? It is now our time to take this responsibility and work together for true repentance and reconciliation.

This is what I felt when I was sitting in a corner during the discussion about who should sing this song: "Putting ourselves in the place of the sinner, we are facilitating true repentance. We may not have killed anyone, but there are some Rwandans who killed, and we are also Rwandans. We need to stand in their place as we all seek God's mercy." When the discussion became very heated and no-one was ready to be the main singer of this song, my brother-in-law Gilbert committed to sing it, but other choir leaders said no because he already had many other responsibilities. So I stood up and said, "Ok, please let me be the one to sing it. I am so ready, I will sing it." But still others started to protest and say, "You?! No! It is not your verse!"

The first time I sang it, someone put her hands up and said, "I am a survivor. Do you want me to say that I killed people? Do you want me to promote that word with singing? I cannot. Please, I will not sing that song. I will sing the rest of the songs but that one is not for me." She pronounced that in the choir, but in the break I approached her outside and said, "You say that you will not sing?" "I cannot. I'm a survivor. They killed my husband! And you want me to sing that I killed them?! No, I will never." And I told her, "Do you think that song is for me?" And she told me, "You must be working for a business. Maybe you are creating a foundation. Maybe you want to get money from mzungus, to get sponsored, because you are singing that song." And I told her, "No. This song will have a powerful message when I sing it, and people will realise that I'm a genocide survivor who has chosen to stand with the perpetrators for the benefit of our community's restoration. This song will have a strong message for all of us, so I have to sing it, to let people – and especially those who killed – realise how much they need God's gift of true repentance, and to help them believe in true forgiveness." And she told me, "David, do you realise what you are saying?" "Yes, I do! I'm a genocide survivor, my dad was killed by Hutus. So I'm from the same background as you, but I'm choosing to go over to that side because I feel a responsibility to help others to experience the power of repentance and forgiveness." And she told me, "You are crazy. Maybe we can take you to hospital. You are not normal. Something has happened to your mind." And I told her, "Just wait. Within two or three days, you will realise that this song is for you. It is not for the benefit of an individual; it is for all of us." Two days before the concert, she came to me and told me, "David, I will sing that song." I asked her why and she said, "I felt convicted by the Holy Spirit of God that I am also responsible for the reconciliation process in this country." This is what she told me.

I started to experience the power of this song when, after our final practice, a pastor's wife, a survivor, requested to be given some time to share something. She told us, "When we were singing this song, I received the energy to forgive the person who killed my father. This song has a powerful message. We have to sing it". The choir members had still not come to an understanding about it, with some saying, "We don't have to sing it," and others saying, "No, please, we have to sing it. It has a helpful message." And then that lady stood up again and said, "Because of these songs, I forgive the person who killed my father – something that I haven't been able to do for the last 20 years. So please, think about this song and sing it, heartily." Some colleagues from a Hutu background were quiet because they thought, "This song is speaking for us. The message is for us. Even if we are not the actual ones who killed, this sin was perpetrated in our historical name, 'Hutu'. It is our relatives, friends and neighbours who killed Tutsis." They were slightly ashamed to see how I quickly committed to standing in their place, representing them, singing out loud those things that are heavily hidden in their hearts. They kept quiet; they didn't say anything. But some genocide survivors were saying, "No, this song is good!" And others: "No, this song is not good! No, we are reconciled. We have forgiven and our President has proclaimed forgiveness to them." But I said again, "Yes, I have forgiven, but there are still some killers in prison and in our communities who silently need forgiveness, and especially God's gift of true repentance. They still need to be encouraged and accompanied into this process in order to be totally saved. They have to participate actively in the process of reconciliation. They need to be forgiven after a genuine action of repentance." We prayed and closed that day's session.

Over the next two days, all of the people came and said, "Oh, this song is good. This song is beautiful." Combining the music of it with the words, they ended up loving it: "It's a good song, it's a good song, it's a good song." And they presented it. After the concert, we had a kind of meeting to discuss the event: How was that? Do you think we can stay and continue this vision? Most of them said, "Please, president," – they were addressing our choir president – "Please, don't go beyond this plan. Keep this. Take it to the whole country. Even if we finish in Rwanda, go to the whole world. We are ready to contribute." We were complaining about having to contribute too much money for the last event, but this year, we are ready to give whatever you need, but keep this plan. It is from God. It is not from people. We are now 100% sure that this is a message from God. Please, we are ready. Let us go to the whole country. We are now committed, 100%." If you told them, "Everyone has to give 1,000,000 RF per year to this project," they would, because they are now committed. They understand what they are doing, they are willing to do that, and they know the impact it is having on society.

DEVOTA

Maybe you could tell me a bit about your experiences during the genocide, and then how you got involved with HWEC at the beginning, when Rhiannon came, and how the workshops and reconciliation work has impacted you?

My name is Devota. During the genocide, I had two kids. I was in the eastern province, in Nyamata. The genocide came in an unexpected way, and that's why all the things that we experienced during the genocide shocked us, and we were surprised. The greatest thing that shocked me was to lose all of my kids and my family. Especially my kids. I lost many members of my family, including my kids. I had no hope for life. I went through difficult moments and unexpected things because, during the genocide, there were just massacres, and they were cutting people. They even tried to burn me in my house, and by God's grace and God's miracle, I survived. That was after my kids' death. They cut them into pieces. They even cut me.

That was a really hard life. I was hidden somewhere, waiting for my last breath. It was then that they burned the house I was in. That was the second house, because they had destroyed my first home and removed the roof and everything. I was hidden there by my friends, who took me there to rest, while I waited for death. I don't know, really, how to define or to explain it, but it really was the will of God. I cannot imagine how I survived, because I left that house while I was not able to move. I was almost dead, because they beat me and I was ripped, hurt and cut. I was almost dead.

I was beaten after I was found, just where I was sleeping. When those people found me there, they beat me, which was really hard. That's why I say that it was God's miracle and grace, because I couldn't imagine that, after all those things that happened to me, I could survive. It was very strange because I couldn't imagine that I could leave that burning house, because I couldn't. I had spent two weeks there and I couldn't even stand up, or sit down. It was a miracle that I could get out.

After that time, I was in a lot of pain, because I was somewhere in the forest where I couldn't see any other person, and no doctor. I was alone in that forest. It was very hard to find a place where you could hide yourself, because it was in mid-April, right at the beginning of the genocide. Besides the house, the other place that you could hide in was the forest, in the waters, with all that pain. Being in the forest, and in the water, with that open wound, it started to attract maggots: they started to grow up in those wounds.

Even at the time of liberation, when the RPF came to redeem the country, it was very hard. They couldn't reach the place where I was because it was very far from the city. It was not easy for me. I cannot say exactly how long I was there, because I was almost dead. I would estimate that it was between the 7th April to the 26th May.

When others were brought back to the city after the liberation of the country, I was hidden in the forest with some of my family, and they were waiting for me to die. One morning in May, we heard a voice, someone calling. He was looking for people, and we recognised the voice, and even the people that he was looking for. Some of the people that we were with went to look for him, and they found that it was a soldier who had come to see if anyone was still alive. That was when we realised that the country had been redeemed.

It was very hard to take me out of that forest because I couldn't even move. They didn't have any way to carry me from there to the town, so they just carried me on a sheet until we got to the hospital. Even then, it was like my life was about to end. Even the doctors didn't know what to do with me, with my pouring pain and wounds.

From then until 2013, I just survived by washing the wound and taking antibiotics. That's all the doctors could do. My wound scared people, even when they weren't looking directly at me. In 2013, I found a doctor who did the surgery, and now I just try to cover the scar. My ear was also cut into two pieces, and that same doctor was even able to operate on my ear.

So now, we get to the second part: how I met Rhiannon. It was in 1995. She used to come to my church. She was with Pastor

Mirakamanse, and she asked me if she could come to my house, and she told me that she wanted to ask me for forgiveness. She began to ask for forgiveness because she had given her testimony in my church, and afterwards, she had realised that there was someone with a very terrifying testimony, which is more powerful than hers. In her testimony, she used to say that she had been through many troubles, but at least she still has siblings and other things, but then she realised that there was a person who doesn't even have siblings anymore. From that moment on, I saw Rhiannon as a special person.

I live in just a one-room house, and it was not even mine. She asked me to stay with her from 8am to 5pm, and we spent the whole day sharing, and I gave her my testimony. Her humility – just accepting me, sitting with me all that time – it really touched my heart. From that time, I saw Rhiannon as a special person too. Many years passed between then and the time that I eventually attended the workshop. I didn't go straight away.

I attended the first healing workshop in 2003, and it brought about a big transformation in my heart. I saw a big change in my life. I couldn't even accept who I was. I was always wondering why this happened to me. Why? Why? I was a Christian, born again, and I couldn't enjoy life here. I was expecting to have full joy only in heaven. I didn't have a desire to have a good life here. My daily prayer was just: "God, take me from this world." All the things I was doing to serve God were just a price that I would pay for God to take me out of this world.

The first thing that touched my heart in the workshop was the topic about how God is able to receive our pain. I didn't know where to take my pain; I couldn't find a place to take it. From the moment that I realised that Jesus is my pain-bearer, I felt released, and my hope – the hope of living – was brought back to me. I felt that I was alive, and I had hope for the future. From that point on, I started to enjoy serving God. And because of that conversation I had with Rhiannon, she became like my closest friend, and even now, she's still a close friend to me. Even today, when I read the book that she wrote, I realise how great the work of God is through her, how big that work is for the country. From that moment, I also became one of the people who brings healing to others, who goes and tells other people that there is a God who can bear their pain. This is my work, this is my ministry; it's what I do.

I'm so happy. From all the bad things that I went through, God has redeemed that pain into something good, and now I have hope for the future. Amen!

That was my story, and you are free to ask me any questions that you want, because I tried to summarise.

Thank-you so much for talking about your story and sharing things that are painful to talk about.

What made you decide to go to the workshop?

It was very hard for me. I couldn't find the interest or see the importance of going to that workshop. But Pastor Joseph, and other people that they were working with, they just came close to me and begged me to go and attend that workshop.

Can you tell me more about the work that you do now?

I live here, in Kigali. I am a preacher in my church. I spend a lot of my time teaching the word of God. There are many people who trust me, and they come to me to share their pain, and I help those people to be released, using the word of God. Those people who are wounded, they are in our churches, and I am very sensitive to those people. I can look at them and recognise them because I also lived in that situation. I just find a strategy, an approach, that I can use to reach that person. And bit by bit, I reach her, and we have a conversation, until she gets healed.

Do you find that one of the big obstacles to forgiveness is that people feel like that means that what happened to them, and their pain, doesn't matter?

I think that is one of the obstacles, but it is not the main one. According to my testimony, this is what I was starting to talk about, that the main challenge is that people don't know the importance of forgiving. When people realise how it is helpful for them to forgive, they forgive. It becomes easy for them to forgive, when they discover how helpful it is for them, not for the people they forgive.

When Rhiannon came, and the HWEC workshops started, was there a difference in communities straight away, or was it a slower process?

It is a journey. It was a process. It was not something that came and people got released right away. It was just a process: bit by bit.

Thank-you. It was very nice to meet you and speak to you. It is powerful to hear stories of coming to a point where you can find release from your woundedness, and find reconciliation and peace, and feel hopeful about life again. So thank-you very much.

I want to thank you. I can see that you are young. I am wondering how you are able to receive all these painful stories. It was a very painful story, and scary. My prayer is that God will help you as you are doing this, and the fact that you are doing this as a Christian, we know that God will use that resource to reach many people. We hope for great healing to many people through what you are doing. Amen!

Thank-you. Amen!

ELIA

My name is Elia. I live here. My home is nearby, but this is where we do our work. Thank-you, because you are touched by our stories. The stories we gave in the DVD: we did not imagine them, they are real stories. But we were blessed that God touched our hearts, and that's why we can confess them. I was telling my brother here that we should maybe sit somewhere safe, because some people do not want to listen to those stories any longer. Some hear them and they are touched by them, but some do not want to step back into that bad history anymore. This is a restaurant, so when you see clients and customers passing by, don't be bothered by them.

So you wanted to meet us because you have heard our stories? I am one of the criminals who perpetrated the genocide. I take the responsibility, I do not blame others, because no-one influenced me: it was my heart that did it. If you guys were grown-ups in '94, maybe you were listening to a television, or to the news, about what was happening here? Well I'm one of those people who was committing genocide.

But things have a source, things have an origin, in order for them to be as strong as they were. I got it from my parents. I like having conversations with people who are of the age to have children, I like telling them my story, because I don't want them to go through the same things I did. I got it from my grandmother, on my father's side. Although she was an old woman, she would teach me that Tutsis, that tribe, are very, very evil people. So I grew up with that conception that they are very bad people, that they are people who should not even be given a chance to live.

I was looking after my father's cows. When we would meet other Tutsis in that field, we would beat them and mistreat them. When '94 came, we did not hold back, we just entered the killings, and I killed; I mean, I really killed people. But the time came when the killings were over, and then we fled the country. But, for me, it wasn't possible to flee. It was practically possible because I was among the first people who got to Gisenyi – Gisenyi is a bordering province, up north – but my heart would not agree with me. I thought about two things: "Why did I kill people?" and, "Me, I'm fleeing death." Then I turned back and I said, "I should not run away from death. I should face the same thing as I did to others."

In those days, I could not find peace. Wherever I would sit, I would not find peace. I remember, it was about 3pm, and I heard a voice, asking me, "Why did you have to kill those people? What did they do to you?" And I couldn't find the answer because I was not even able to see the one who was asking me. But what followed was just cries: just tears, many tears. At some point, I just cried out and started repenting, asking God for forgiveness, telling God: "Just forgive me, because I did wrong to you." From that point, I made a decision that if anyone should ask me about what I have done or what I have witnessed, I would just tell them my story without beating around the bush. So I can receive you now. I could have told my brother here, "No, no. I'm busy. I'm not available."

A time came when I was caught and put in prison. But I was blessed that, after sometime, a law was passed that anyone who chose to confess might be forgiven. That law helped me, because it emphasised the decision I had taken. In prison, to confess what you have done was not easy, but that law gave me a platform. I was given a chance to confess, and then there followed the presidential pardon, and I found myself outside prison. After they announced to me that I would be released, it troubled me, because I was wondering, "How am I going to face this society? The same people that I have wronged?" God is amazing. He knows how to turn bad into good.

I came out and I arrived here. The first friends that I met were the same people whose family I had killed. It was not false, or just a smile to cover up something hidden inside; those friends were my neighbours. My brother knows them and has met them. I really took a major role in killing their siblings, but God just connected us and now we are a team, healing the hearts of Rwandans. One thing is amazing: I had a wedding. Before the genocide, I had taken a wife but in an illegal way. But after I got saved, I had to legalise my marriage, so we got married legally. What is amazing is that the bridesmaids were the same people, the victims, whose family I had killed. Now we are living peacefully with them. When I need money,

I can go and borrow from them. When they need money, I can give it to them when I have it. If I need a bicycle to use, then they have it. And if I have it, and they need it, I just lend it to them.

So we started going around this country, all over the country, with those people: them telling their stories and me telling mine. They tell how they experienced forgiveness. I can say that it's still an ongoing journey. I also hear that it's travelling even beyond the borders of the country. Like you guys: it reached you, and that's why you have come. That's our wish: that it will go beyond borders, to reach people who have gone through the same things as Rwandans, and maybe our stories can help.

Thank-you for receiving.

Thank-you so much.

Did you get saved when you were in prison, or after you came out of prison?

Even before the genocide, I was kind of saved, but I was among those people in charge who are not really saved inside. For example, when the preacher was from the Tutsi tribe, I would not agree to help. So I did not have salvation really. I would say that I got saved when I started hearing the voice. It was the first time I heard God, and at that time God fulfilled all the vows I had made. In that place, where I was just shedding tears, I vowed to God: "If you keep me from dying, I will serve you." Dying was very easy, and very possible, for many people were taking revenge. I can say that my journey of salvation started at that time, and is still ongoing.

Can I ask you about the Gacaca, and how that helped the process of justice and forgiveness?

The Gacaca came to give a platform for people to be heard to confess their crimes, to publicly apologise to the victims. I would say that the criminals made Gacaca possible, because if the criminals would not open their hearts to admit their crimes, Gacaca would never have been possible. We were like the keys to Gacaca, to this access of Gacaca, and now we can see the fruits. Gacaca gave us a platform.

When we look at Rwanda and what happened, and the reconciliation that has happened since, what do you think we need to learn?

The reconciliation that happened in this country is not supposed to be a mystery to outsiders. It is something tangible; it's a real life story that actually happened. When you do research, or a survey, from '94 until now, and compare how Rwandans who were living together in '94 can, even now, live together: without adding anymore words, that's a big lesson in itself. Even the fact that no-one, now, is taking revenge on his neighbours, and just going to kill them because they have killed his family members: that's a miracle by itself. It's a big lesson. So if the whole world is looking at Rwanda, they should learn a big lesson. I should now be living in fear. I should be afraid to go into the forest for fear of meeting a relative of the guy I killed, but now I don't have that fear, and what made that possible was the reconciliation that happened between the Rwandan people. That's the answer I can give you.

What was it like coming back to this place, where you live, and meeting your neighbours again?

I have jumped that part, but thank-you for bringing it up. When I was released from prison, I was not free. They could greet me but I didn't trust them. I thought, "Maybe that's a trick to get hold of me."

To hurt you.

Yes. I had my one family member, my sister, and she lent me money so that I could make a life. I was selling flowers and small fish in the market, and I could see that many of my customers were from those families, my victims. So I could not trust them, but I could see them approaching me, just freely. Then I started thinking: "Maybe it's not from a true heart, but by their words at least I can see that they are more free than me." With time, I started cooling down, just getting used to living with them. What I can confess now – the way I just brought out my story – was not possible at that time.

One day, the African Evangelistic Enterprise organised a seminar. At that time, it was Pastor Nyamutera Joseph that they were working with. They had organised a seminar in our province, just nearby here. I was invited, and I was blessed to see that those people I had hurt were also invited. There were about 72 of us. The seminar started – the first day, the second day – but as they were teaching us, it felt like they were taking a long time. I started feeling like I was bursting. I wanted them to give me a chance to get out what was filling me. Then they taught us a lesson called, "To stand in the gap." I did not come forward to stand in the gap and accept the gap for myself, but I took that chance to just get out what was filling my heart. I started confessing right away. I apologised for my people, my tribe, who are still in denial. I can say that the journey of confessing and reconciliation started at that time, at that seminar. The place became small and crowded because they were just standing up and hugging me, and another one was taking my arm, because there were so many wanting to hug me. I felt released, like a burden lifted off me, and the cloud of fear and mistrust was just gone. So I've started opening myself up freely now. That's how it started, in short.

Do you remember when that seminar was?

It was in 2003. I can't remember the month, but I had just been released.

I wanted to ask something else, if that's ok?

It's ok, but also give me some time; I want to ask you something.

How do you find being back in the community now, even though you are reconciled? Is it still difficult, and what are the challenges that you face?

The consequences cannot be avoided, because everyone who was in this country had to face the consequences, the challenges. Now there is this programme of paying back: restitution to the victims of the genocide. So it has to have a consequence, financially, to the family, because I'm working to pay them back. I am also struggling to take care of my family, so it's tricky. And survivors of the genocide, also, are living with a challenge because, financially, they are supposed to be at a certain level, but they are not, because of us, so we are struggling to pay back. Even just now, that person who just left here: I gave him 5000 RF. But the blessing I have is that we understand each other. We agree. I tell them, "This is my level, financially, so allow me to pay you back month by month," and they agree. To give you an example, there is a person to whom I owe 200,000 RF in total. But because of that unity, he just accepts whatever I have. Yes, that's a challenge. Thank-you.

Can I ask you a question? The fact that you left your country to come here to Rwanda is because you are touched by our stories. So I want to ask you, when you go back to your country, what will you make of our testimonies? Because, everywhere in the world, there are conflicts. So do you play a role in resolving those conflicts, using our testimonies, or what do you use our testimonies for?

Partly, I am collecting them together to write a story with Joseph Nyamutera to make these stories more accessible to people who are working in situations of conflict that need healing.

Yes, to tell the story of what God has been doing, and the healing and reconciliation that has been happening in Rwanda. Because people know lots of what happened during the genocide, but they need to know what's happened since. They need to know. It's a very powerful message.

That's the only question I have: "These people are asking us about our stories, what do they make of them? What do they use them for?" That's the same question I ask everyone.

So, may God help you to make that project a success. Another wish I would express is that after the publication of that book, after it is written by knowledgable people, you can also give us a copy, so that we can read our own stories.

We will make sure Joseph and Mercy Ministries have lots of copies that they can give out to people.

Many people like you come to ask us questions, and maybe they are organising, or preparing, a movie or a documentary, but we never watch those movies. So my wish is that they would come to show us the movie in which we played a part, and maybe it would also help others who are still covering up, who are still ashamed, to open up, and to be more free.

Has he seen the documentary?

Translator: Yes, he's seen it, and he is among the people who gave a testimony, and this is our responsibility. I think, in March, we'll give him the DVD, because we want to give it with a purpose. We don't want people to have it for the sake of having it. So we'll maybe say to people, "This is the DVD. What do you think? Do you think it can help in your community?" Then we follow them. Because it is a sensitive DVD. Then we can have feedback, and we can give advice and support, in order to make it something which can bring change, not something for entertainment.

Elia: It would help us, because the national mourning is in April, so it would help a lot. Thank-you.

Thank-you so much.

ODETTE

We're very interested to hear the stories of people who have been able to find healing from wounds, and reconciliation, through the HWEC workshops, and to hear about the powerful things that God has been doing to heal and bring hope to people.

Obviously, you were at the first HWEC workshop, so we would like to hear about that and how you found it. So maybe you could tell us a bit about your background, so we can start to understand how you were wounded, and talk about the workshop, and what impact that had?

Thank-you. It's good that people are now getting to know our stories, and it also gives glory to God, because really, we give all the credit to God. Because my history personally, or our history as a nation, has not been good at all. We had a conflict in our nation that we experienced, we endured; a genocide that wounded our hearts tremendously. During the '94 genocide, I was not around here; I was staying in the north. Because of my husband's work, we would move around a lot. So the genocide hit me at home with my kids, but my husband was not around; he was in Kigali for work. I should tell you that they killed all of my children. I spent a lot of time hiding in the bush, and my heart was swollen, because there is a difference between being wounded and having a swollen heart. At the beginning of the genocide, it didn't seem like a big thing, a big deal. I think that, had it not been for God, or for God's people coming and assisting us, nobody would be alive today. No genocide victim would still be alive.

So I spent a lot of time in the bush, to the point that, from leaning on one side, I got crippled. I have a handicap on my right shoulder, there, because I was just lying in the same position. Snakes were passing over me, and there was the sound of guns. I could not move, because I was hiding. I was lying in that bush, knowing that all of my kids had been tortured and killed. So even my brain was not functioning well. I spent between three weeks and a month there, in that bush, and I did not eat anything, because I didn't have the peace of mind to find my appetite.

I was the only one left standing in our village and everyone, every criminal, was looking for me, so I had to leave that place and run away, because I was hearing rumours that, if they caught the person who was hiding me, they would force that person to kill me, and they would also charge that person money. So I left that place, heading nowhere; just wandering the streets like a mad person, without knowing where I was going. The current army found me on the main road, with no sound mind.

Those people who were looking for me were planning to crucify me. Now, on the main road, as I was running away from the bush, I met a friend of my family. He took me home, but his wife was afraid and said, "If they catch us hiding this person, they are going to kill us as well as her." So that couple took me to someone else's, who was a family friend. In his home, there were a lot of people who had run away [from the RPF], so he said, "I cannot mix you with these people. I don't want these people to see you." So he took some sheeting, a plastic tent, and he prepared a place in the trash. He prepared a place for me to hide, and he also made a shortcut in the backyard of his home, for me to be able to go outside without going through the gate.

I spent four days in that hiding place. Then [the RPF] took the area. I remember seeing them come rushing into the house, telling me, "Oh, now this area has been captured. We know they cannot do anything to you, so maybe you will wait to be freed, but we have to flee." So they said: "Just wait here, for [the RPF] to get to you, and if we come back, that's fine. If we don't, you will be safe because they will surely get to you." So, after they had run away, I spent another two days in that house, alone.

I waited in that house, alone. I was in a bad state: my hair was a mess and I had not bathed for a long, long time. I just waited there, hiding in one of the rooms, with my Bible in my hands. The person whose house I was in had told me not to close the gate and the door. So I waited.

After two days, I heard that there was a lot of fighting outside: gunshots, and a lot of mess. I heard, outside in the compound, people speaking and getting into the house, and I thought, "It's the end of me now. My killers are in the house." So I prepared myself to die. I did not know that they were [RPF]. They came into the house looking for storehouses. One of them got into one of the rooms, and then when he heard that there was a person in the room, he got ready to shoot. When I saw them – because they had described to me what [RPF] would look like – I saw that it might be them, so I just put my hands in the air and said, "No, no, no, no! I am a survivor of the genocide." I just started telling them the story. They did not want to believe me, but finally one of them said, "Maybe this lady..." They asked me many questions: "Where are you from?" I told them my story. So finally those soldiers decided to help me.

It's a long story, but in short: they took me to Gako military camp, not far from here. After Nyamata, this whole province was caught by [the RPF]. They brought us back here. They took me to an orphanage, and I started asking around about what really happened to my family. I had four children: the firstborn were twins, and two other children. There is no good way of being killed, but they were massacred, they were tortured, and very brutally murdered.

The firstborn: she tried to run away, and she was in this river, trying to swim, and she couldn't. They caught her, and they just cut her with a machete, but she did not die right away. From ten in the morning, until 3pm, she was just fighting between death and life. They came back and said, "She will not live anyway." So she was buried alive. They didn't finish her, they just buried her alive. Two of the others were beaten with a stick that had nails in it. So they were really brutally murdered.

In that orphanage, where I was living, they were taking in many kids that were brought there. Wherever they went, there were kids just in the bushes, in the houses, and they were bringing them to that orphanage for me to help them, and to raise them. I would just spend every day crying because the kids would tell me stories about one of my children, about how they died. Like, the second born: when the genocide started, he was not with us. A family friend had taken him to help us raise him. So they would bring me stories about his death, and I would find myself crying because I was living among these kids, but with no child of my own. It was such a test; it was such a problem. I was just crying every day. I had a lot of tears.

A lot of stories would reach me about my family members, all of them at the same time. My mother was forced to eat her child. So she was killed eating her own child. Then my in-laws were burned alive in their house. The wife of my brother was killed when she was pregnant: she was cut open, and they took the baby out of her. All of those stories are just...

[Translator breaks off]

...Rhiannon, when she came to Rwanda. We were in another place, but later we were called to come and meet her, so that Rhiannon could have an opportunity to talk to us. When she talked to us, she said, "I want to give you this opportunity to cry." She was teaching us to cry, but I resisted, because we were with some Hutu and we are Tutsi. It was the setting: the atmosphere was not good for us to be able to cry. But I kept attending the seminars.

When Rhiannon started to teach about healing, I could see that it was a process. She, herself, could come each day with a different impression. It was at that time that she got this revelation of a flower growing through the ashes. Then she started to use that message to help the people who were around. In myself, I followed that journey. Time after time, I could see that people were being touched by the message.

The main problem I had was that I felt guilty because when my children and I departed, I told the firstborn: "Take the kids! Take your sisters, take your sisters!" So that image of sending her away with the other children had stayed in me. I didn't think much about their father, even though I had heard about the way he was killed too, but the main problem I had was that guilt of sending away my children, and then afterwards finding out how they were killed. It was that issue that was swollen in my heart when I met Rhiannon. So I closed my heart to the messages they were giving us. But the person who got to work inside my heart was Pastor Joseph Mugasa. Because, whenever we would meet, he would sing for me, and I just felt a bit released. So I opened my heart and started to express that anger and bitterness, and that guilt, and started to receive the message.

During those messages and those workshops, the session that helped me a lot was the session of the Holy Nations. When I arrived and I saw the table prepared, and when I saw Pastor Joseph standing together with Rhiannon and Anastase, I just burst: I started crying and shouting, and making such a mess. Then the pastor told us that someone from a different ethnic group should try to comfort me, and then that person came, and he was putting sweets in my mouth, hugging me, and just trying to comfort me. I can say that that was the beginning of the journey of healing, the beginning of the healing process. What happened is that I started receiving inner peace, and I even started to see that forgiving is possible.

After that, there was another workshop, organised by AEE, at another place. I went there, together with other survivors of the genocide, and we came to a time of hugging and embracing the people from the other ethnic group. Then my fellow survivors were mad at me. They said, "You! Ah, they have given you money, for you to go and just hug those killers!" They were calling them all sorts of names. So I said, "No, no, no, me? I'm out to seek peace, so leave me alone. I know what I'm doing." I just grabbed the person and hugged them. So that's what showed me that I had received healing and forgiveness, and that the healing had started in my heart.

Translator: The first person she hugged was the one who betrayed her children. So that's why the other genocide survivors said, "How can you hug someone who betrayed your children, so that they were killed?"

I mean, that person had given her children away to be killed, and she hugged that person. The others could not believe it. They said,

"You must have been given money. You can't be of sound mind. You can't just hug someone who killed your children."

Odette: That person had fled to Congo, and when he came back to the country, he found that I had left the orphanage with kids, with orphans. I received a lot of children in my home. When the church, saw that I had a lot of children in my home and I didn't have means to feed them, they gave me a job. In the shop that they gave me, there was this photocopying machine. Before, I would not receive any customer from the Hutu tribe, because I was so mad at them; I hated them wholeheartedly. When that person came back into the country, he came to the shop. He did not know that I was the one working there, so when he found me he wanted to run. He was afraid, and he started shaking. So, I told him, "No, no, no. I have forgiven you. I have released you. I received messages which helped me to release you in my heart." We sat down and he told me the whole story: how my children were killed, how he abandoned them. He told me the whole journey of my children being killed. We started to cry together, and as I was crying I felt a big, heavy burden being lifted off me, piece by piece. I was crying, and as my tears were coming out of me, I felt that they were bringing out some of the stuff that was in my heart.

I took those people of God to my home town, to take the message to my home community. When we got there, and my former neighbours saw that I was coming with those people, they wanted to run. They thought I was coming to have them cursed or something. But finally, they came and they sat with us. The people of God ministered to them the message of HWEC, and what God did in my home town was amazing! People started confessing, and survivors forgave... It was such a big story of healing and reconciliation.

From that point, I recovered my hope: hope of life was restored back to me. Before, I weighed 42 kgs. I was so thin, because that hatred and that bitterness was eating away all my appetite, and the taste of life, and hope for living. But, after teaching us and giving us that message, they also organised the TOF – the Training of Facilitators – and they taught us how to help others. So, as I was helping others, I was also receiving the full supplement of my healing. I went to many people and I took the message to them. I helped them, and as I was helping them, then also my hope for living was restored back to me, as well as joy, and hope for development: to have that desire to develop, to do better, to work for a better life. Before, I was feeling low, and I didn't think I would have a bright future, but now I have development projects. I can now have visions about my future. Before, I had lost the taste for work, but now I like working again, and I feel like the joy of life was restored back to me.

I haven't mentioned the group of widows that I have helped: they formed an association. So now, I can say that I am receiving full healing. I am so grateful to Rhiannon, who brought us the message. She was like a tool in the hands of God, that God used to heal our inner wounds. Recently, that group of widows invited me to go and teach them. I taught them the message of the session of wounded hearts, because I feel that without your heart first being healed, you cannot get far in life; you cannot really achieve anything tangible in life. So I feel like the process of healing really is going well in life, and in my heart, thanks to Rhiannon.

Now the brief background of this church, here: I've not mentioned it, but they slaughtered a lot of cows in this church; cows for Tutsis that were being killed. A lot of bad things happened. The pastor of this church is in jail now. He was the one leading it, in his own church. That's the background of this place.

Thank-you very much. Thank-you for listening to me. If you have any questions, you can ask.

Thank-you so much.

It was not easy. Someone requested me to write a book, but it's so long that these are just portions of my story. It's very long.

It's really powerful to hear how you were able to forgive the person who betrayed your children, to hug him and forgive him.

The important part is your inner being. Everything happens on the inside. You might be physically still standing, but you are dying inside. So it's only God who did it, really. Without God, I could never be able to forgive that person, but God did it and made the impossible possible. God not only healed my inner person, He also healed my physical person: the shoulder that I had leant on. I was medically checked, and they found that the bones of this area were broken into many pieces. If you saw a picture, you would say that this person would be crippled for life! But God has healed me, and I'm now recovered.

There is another source of joy that God did not take away: my second born was not killed! During the genocide, we were not together. She survived, and she gave me a grandchild. Yes, that also came as a comfort to me. I thought that my family was done, and that I was finished, but seeing that person, my own blood, that little thing, was such a source of comfort.

Omer was telling me that you work as a mediator now. Maybe you can tell us a little bit about that?

In that job – if I may call it a job, because we are not given money but I take it as a ministry from God, because what we do is not very different from the message we received – it helps us a lot in bringing the two conflicting parties together. Many cases of conflict here are land or farm issues, so when I see them coming back together again, and resolving their conflict, they are also a source of joy. This message is a very useful resource for me.

Thank-you so much.

Get Involved

If you have been impacted by this story of healing and reconciliation, please share it with your friends and family. The book is available to buy online at **www.selwynshore.com/books/hope**

Hear more about the book, related projects and events, and how you can support the work of Rabagirana Ministries by signing up to the newsletter at **www.selwynshore.com/books/hope**

Follow the work of Rabagirana Ministries at **www.rabagirana.org**

Find out more about Dr. Rhiannon Lloyd and the HWEC ministry at **www.healingthenations.co.uk**

You can also find We Are One Ministries at **www.weareone.org.uk**